THE
ULTIMATE
Restoring the Culture of Marriage

JONATHAN CLAUSSEN, MD

© 2017 Jonathan Claussen, MD

Published by Family Restoration Publishing
27704 430th Street
Browerville, Minnesota 56438
www.familyrestorationproject.com

Printed in the United States of America

All rights reserved. No portion of this book may be reproduced in any form without permission from the publisher, except as permitted by U.S. copyright law. For permissions contact:

All Biblical references are from the New King James Version and italics are added unless otherwise noted.

Cover and interior graphics by Dawn Williams.

ISBN 978-1974642236

Dedication

This book is dedicated to my precious wife, Amy.

Amy, this book, in many ways, is a celebration of you and your presence in my life. Your journey of love in the embrace of the Father shifted everything. Our love is simply the overflow of His extravagance.

You inspire me, encourage me, and believe in me, and you captivate me.

Actually, you *are* me.

Our adventure together in His kingdom as "one flesh" is the greatest joy in my life!

Endorsements

Jon Claussen has nailed it again! I have known Jon for several years as this message has grown in him and I can say with full confidence that this is a message from God. He has placed His presence in it, His power on it, and His wisdom throughout it. Every time Jon speaks about family, God imparts grace to the hearers to help them do family better, and I know the same will happen for every marriage that makes room for this book. This book is filled with the power of restoration. May the revolution of restoration spread until God's word is fulfilled and the restoration of all things is complete!

Nathanael White
Senior leader of Presence Church
Author of *Become You*

From the moment Jon Claussen so passionately spilled the vision on us that he, and his wife Amy, had foreseen God's original design for the family restored, we were hooked! So impressed were we with the depth of revelation, and his ability to mine out of the scriptures dynamic and timeless truths, that we invited Jon as a main speaker for the International Healing Conference. Jon's message was absolutely transformative, and because of his depth of communicating that revelation, their ministry, the Family Restoration Project, was launched like a rocket!

We had the privilege of being part of their first Marriage Conference, and again we were so blessed to see the transforming power of the Holy Spirit change and heal lives and marriages as the attendees had their identities restored as sons and daughters of their loving Heavenly Father!

We want to highly commend to you Jon's new book, *The Ultimate: Restoring the Culture of Marriage*. It is amazing and full of fresh, exciting revelational teaching! We were blessed beyond measure by his insightful unfolding of God's plan set in the beginning, for the marriage culture of Eden to reflect the culture of heaven, and to see that this includes a co-mission where He infuses His own heart into the hearts of His creation. From this culture it becomes evident that each married couple is not be able to do alone what needs to be done together! Jon's insightful unfolding of the Bible's cultural mandates will help you to have the keys to healthy, vibrant, and indeed *The Ultimate* marriage!

Apostle Jim Rickard and Pastor Ramona Rickard
Founders of RAIN –
Resurrection Apostolic International Network.
Founders of IAHM –
The International Association of Healing Ministries,

My family and I have been so blessed to know the Claussen family over the past several years. So it was no surprise that when I started to read through *The The Ultimate: Restoring the Culture of Marriage,* that it was difficult to put down. The stories, the insights and the profound revelation in this book come from a place of deep authentic devotion and intimacy with Abba. Jonathan has so beautifully and creatively communicated the Biblical perspective of marriage in a way that is relevant and very much needed in Today's culture. After reading *The Ultimate...* our marriage has received an upgrade!

Jon Russell
Worship leader, Time to Revive
Hosanna! Church

As a single person who plans to be married someday, I can't recommend this book enough! *The Ultimate* bypasses the symptoms of issues and gets right to the heart of the matter; how we relate to Father God to meet our needs and one another out of that overflow. The truths contained in these pages (much like learning to count, the alphabet, or the primary colors) are both simple and yet extremely profound. These practical and life-changing principles are applicable to people in all seasons of life, whether single or married, and form a solid foundation from which one can build a great life and marriage upon. If believers truly took to heart and lived out these values we would see society significantly transformed in even just one generation! Get this book, give it as a gift to your friends, and read it again and again.

Kristen D'Arpa
Founder of i Go Glocal
Author of *Kingdom Culture School of Ministry*

The Ultimate: Restoring the Culture of Marriage is a readily available pocket-size conference on marriage! The Family Restoration Project has transformed families and marriages in our church for the last few years. Marriages headed towards divorce have been saved through the content this book contains. *The Ultimate: Restoring the Culture of Marriage* is an anointed NOW message that unpacks the true foundation of what the Biblical marriage is all about.

Stephen Ekholm
Lead Pastor, Living Hope Church
Mora, MN

I've known Jonathan and Amy for several years now, have heard them speak at conferences, and have had them minister at my local church. I've seen how their ministry has transformed lives where other marriage ministries have failed. These marriages were changed because what is offered is not the same old performance-based principles that only weigh people down with more guilt over their failure. No, they convey a fresh understanding of ancient truths not only found in Scripture but also in relationship with Papa God, who changes us from the inside-out with His love, which in turn, transforms how we love. Those same transformational truths are found in this book.

The Ultimate: Restoring the Culture of Marriage cuts right to the heart of what is needed for marriages to not only survive but flourish as God originally intended. Jonathan surgically goes after the cancerous myths that are killing so many marriages, using popular song titles to tie important truths together about God's intended cultural design for marriage. I highly recommend you get this book! Read it, understand it, and live it. You won't regret it!

Mel Wild
Author of *Sonshift*
Senior Pastor of Cornerstone Church
Prairie du Chien, WI

Jonathan Claussen's book on marriage, *The Ultimate,* lays the foundation for what God meant for every marriage...a marriage made in heaven. God intended man and woman, in marriage, to embrace each other as equals, friends, and deep lovers; a marriage full of purpose, synergy and harmony. This book reveals God's design for a great marriage, with each couple then building their unique story on top of this important foundation.

Paul and Maralee Gazelka
Together in marriage ministry,
business, politics, and arts

Foreword

When someone sets out to write a book about marriage, it's important that they really know what they're talking about. Let me just say this from the start, Jon Claussen really knows what he's talking about!

There are too many marriage self-help books out there that address actions and behavior, yet never get to the core of God's heart on the matter. His book, *The Ultimate*, is an amazing book that is filled with more than just requirements for a good marriage. It literally goes back to the Genesis of marriage and rewrites how we see marriage through the eyes of God.

I've known Jon, his wife Amy, and their wonderful family for a number of years now and what I think everyone, including me, takes away after being with them is this, "I would love to have been raised by them!" They carry God's heart in a way that makes you feel the very presence of God. When you look into their eyes you get the feeling that God's looking back. I know that sounds a little corny, but if you ever get the chance to do it you'll understand.

The Ultimate is just that. It's a journey to a summit of truth. As you read this wonderful book you begin to see things about love, relationships and marriage that you've never seen before. Like that moment when you've been hiking and you take those last few steps over the ridge and suddenly see the vista, you will experience a view that will take your breath away.

A few years ago I was ministering in Minnesota and had the wonderful privilege of leading worship at, and attending a marriage seminar (from where this book originates) put on by Jon and Amy. It was there that I began to fully see the impact that they have and will continue to have on others because of how they live their lives. Their children were a vital part of everything. They were an important part of my worship team and they served in every area during that weekend.

It's one thing to have your children like you, even love you, but it's quite another thing to have your children want to be around you...constantly. Their kids (who are wonderful by the way) absolutely loved being around their parents. That speaks! They minister together and they are each other's biggest cheerleaders.

As you read *The Ultimate*, you begin to see what created this amazing family dynamic. It's rooted in the revelation of value and identity. When someone is valued, they take on a Godly identity. That's what Jon has received directly from the Lord and that is what he has passed on to his children, and as you read this book you will be invited into that same revelation.

As a medical doctor, Jon knows what it means to study and learn. Fortunately for us, he has applied that same tenacity to the study of God's word. We are its beneficiaries. Jon's theological treatise is solid and his love for history is infectious. On a natural level, this is a very enjoyable book.

There are a few more points that I want to highlight. As I was reading *The Ultimate*, chapter after chapter I said to myself, "This chapter alone is worth the price of the book." I often say that when I'm reading a book but very rarely do I say it over and over again. Jon has received some incredible insight into the power of an orphan spirit and through this book he brings hope to those who suffer its effect. His chapter on submission was eye opening. He may shake up a few "starched" believers when he addresses this subject, but personally…I loved it! His prescription (remember now, he is a doctor) as to how we can heat up the bedroom is genius.

If you've just picked up this book and are wondering if you should buy it, let me simply say this. Don't! Buy 10 copies, because once you've read it you will want to give a copy to everyone you know.

This may be a simple read but in no way is this a simple book. It is bathed in prayer, rooted in truth, delivered in love, and filled with God's heart. You will do yourself and everyone you know a great service by reading and applying the life found within the pages of Jon Claussen's book, *The Ultimate*.

Thank you, Jon, for all the hours you've given to bring this book to life. From your years of marriage, your spectacular seminars, and now this great book, you have drawn on the heart and wisdom of God and given the Body of Christ (and any lover of love and truth) *The Ultimate* gift.

Chris DuPré
Writer, pastor, speaker
Author of The Wild Love of God

Contents

Introduction: "The First Time Ever I Saw Your Face"..................11

Chapter 1: "Another Day in Paradise"....................18

Chapter 2: "The Way We Were"..............................31

Chapter 3: "I Still Haven't Found What I'm Looking For"....45

Chapter 4: "Happy Together"...................................61

Chapter 5: "How Am I Supposed to Live Without You"..........73

Chapter 6: "Help!" (I Need Somebody)..............................83

Chapter 7: "Bridge Over Troubled Water"..............................97

Chapter 8: "Say You, Say Me"...............................109

Chapter 9: "Leader of the Pack"...........................125

Chapter 10: "How Deep Is Your Love".....................136

Chapter 11: "If You Don't Know Me by Now".......................150

Conclusion: "Get Back" (to Where You Once Belonged)........165

*All of the chapter titles are named after the "ultimate" song of the year according to *Billboard*'s "No. 1 Hits."

Introduction

"The First Time Ever I Saw Your Face"

Roberta Flack, 1972

I remember the first time ever I saw her face. Upon our engagement in 1994, my soon-to-be wife, Amy, and I wrote down our stories of how we met so we would never forget, knowing that someday our children would want to read them. Here are some excerpts:

One Sunday when I was singing up front...it happened. I was returning to my seat when we were done, and my usual glance at Amy was returned by a glance from her. It was special; our eyes really did meet. The glance brought about the following effects: my heart temporarily stopped, my knees buckled, my collar felt too tight, and from then on Amy was permanently stuck in my mind.

I remember standing to worship and looking up to the front of the church. I saw a handsome young man in a very striking forest-green suit standing and singing to the Lord. While I observed him from afar, that pair of eyes turned and looked in my direction. After a few seconds, it became clear that we were looking at each other. My heart was beating a bit faster than normal, and excitement was welling up inside of me as we exchanged glances.

In our case, it happened to be love at first sight. Like most young couples, we were wide-eyed and very much in love. We also didn't fully appreciate and understand everything that goes into a relationship, especially marriage.

Our marriage, in most respects, has been one of joy and wonderment, and, as sappy as it sounds, we seem to fall more in love with each other every day. Unlike so many other marriages, our relationship is not defined by hurt and disillusionment. Not that we have never hurt each other or felt disillusioned in our marriage, but, by any internal or external measurement, one could easily conclude that our marriage is a good one. The problem is, until just a few years prior to writing this book, we didn't have a full understanding of what *good* is, and we didn't fully understand what *marriage* is.

Based upon our Western, academic thinking, "good" usually means "better than everyone else." We tend to have a "grading on the curve" mentality. I never cheated on my wife. I never struck her in anger. I very rarely raised my voice. Most of the time, we speak respectfully to each other. We try to have a regular date night. We both love the Lord with our whole hearts, and we both turn to Him in times of conflict.

We attempt to raise our children with mutual understanding, and we are affectionate toward each other in words and actions. This list alone, when compared to all other marriages, adds up to a pretty good marriage...when grading on the curve.

As my passion for family and marriage grew, I quickly realized that the book of Genesis is fundamental; it is the platform for the remaining pieces of scripture. I also realized that marriage seems to be the central focus of scripture, even from the beginning.

I remember my dad exhorting our family to restore the word "good." When the heavenly Father creates something, in His infinite wisdom and ability, He sees all that He has made and calls it good. When my dad shared this truth, and I explored this further, I realized *my* good was not the same as *His* good. I also realized, *my* idea of marriage was not *His* original idea for marriage. I discovered, through the dust and erosion of time, we had lost the original heart of the Father.

In many respects, I may be the perfect person to write this book on marriage. Amy and I had parents and grandparents who were all married for over fifty years, provided Christian homes, and passed on that loving inheritance to us. We were both raised in environments where loving marriages were demonstrated and normal. I never once went to bed as a child with the fear that divorce would knock on our family's door. I never once went to bed at night feeling unloved or unaccepted. Subsequently, I have never gone to bed at night with the fear that my own marriage will end, and I continue to feel loved and accepted.

Despite this upbringing and solid foundation, I am convinced that there is a deeper revelation of truth. I discovered that we have misunderstood many things, we have been insulated by wrong theology, and believed outright lies in regard to love, marriage, and intimacy. If someone like me, with every relational and educational advantage, could be blind to the truth, it could happen to anyone. There is an ancient truth that needs to be uncovered.

Mark Twain said, "It ain't what you don't know that gets you into trouble. It's what you know for sure that just ain't so." This book exposes many things about marriage that I had "known for sure" but discovered that it "just ain't so!" This discovery may "ruffle some feathers" and I'm OK with that as long as His heart, His truth, and His word are declared! I wasn't looking for a new or fresh angle to create a stir or give you something new to talk about. I simply went back to the beginning.

If your marriage is in shambles, and you need a complete reset, a new direction, a new hope, then this book is for you.

If you feel that you have a solid marriage, but there seems to be something missing—perhaps you feel you are drifting apart, and there is a loss of intimacy—then this book is for you.

If you feel like you have a *relatively* good marriage, but you are open to the greater depth of intimacy that can only be found in the Author of all things, then this book is for you.

If you are a teenager, a single adult, or an engaged couple, and you want to start your relationships with the knowledge that took me over forty years to discover, then this book is for you.

Our God is a God of restoration, and He not only looks to restore marriages but also desires to restore its purpose and destiny.

In this book, you will learn that marriage is established in the Garden of Eden as a demonstration of heaven. Because of this, I realized that diminishing the significance of my marriage is diminishing heaven itself. Family is the Father's original plan and marriage is the crowning demonstration of His "good".

You will discover the crafty plan to bring separation between our loving Father and us and see how that orphan spirit is still present today in marriages and families. You will rejoice at how our covenantal Father and His obedient Son ushered in the times of restoration that provide hope for humankind and every relationship.

With the culture of Eden back in play, we can bravely explore the original heart of the Father in every marriage. We can restore the depths of intimacy that have been there for us since the beginning of time. Adam and Eve do not have to be the sole married couple to walk in the "naked and unashamed" culture of Eden. Through the blood of Jesus, the culture—the very heart of the Father—is once again afforded to us!

There is more good news. I believe this is just the beginning of a family movement. I believe the Father is summoning forth a revival that will quickly and effectively change the culture among families and marriages. We are after the culture that changes hearts, because changed hearts restore families, and restored families go on to change and affect the culture of society.

In order to change the culture and bring restoration to marriages, we can't have another book that is simply a to-do list. The *Seven Things You Can Do to Save Your Marriage,* the *Five Ways to Re-Spark Romance,* or *Tips for Taking Your Spouse Out on a Date* have value and should be given our attention, but none of these will bring restoration. Action lists or checked boxes may provide a needed discipline to a marriage, but they will not change hearts. I'm confident that this book will not put more weight on your shoulders by burdening you with trying to fix your own marriage. Only the Holy Spirit can inspire real transformation and restoration. If you are tired and worn out from having to try harder, then please embrace this message and simply rest in His truth. His truth will set you free!

I am aware that this may sound a bit like one of those late-night diet infomercials, the ones that promise you will lose weight without any effort at all, but I am not making that type of claim. Any relationship requires effort and commitment, but the Father wants us to always approach this world from a place of rest and identity.

That is our testimony. Amy and I have found a new freedom, a new energy, and a new peace in our marriage. We did not find it by our own effort or by working harder. We found it in our identity—as sons and daughters of the Father—by discovering what it means to be married. We are on this exciting journey of uncovering the greater depths of intimacy, and you can too. We are no longer satisfied with a marriage that the world deems good. We are restoring a culture of marriage that He created and He calls good! We will settle for nothing less than the ultimate.

1

"Another Day in Paradise"
Phil Collins, 1989

To begin our journey to the greater depths of intimacy in marriage, we need to start at the beginning. This book is not simply a collection of my good ideas about marriage but rather a discovery of the Father's good idea about marriage. He laid out His culture for marriage and family at the very beginning.

As we start, we need to keep a single focus in mind: restoration. God is a God of restoration. He is also a God that never goes back on His word or plans for His people. He created a loving culture for His children and that culture is captured in the book of Genesis.

If the focus is restoration, then we need to know two things before we begin pursuing restoration. Imagine you were starting a renovation project, perhaps restoring an old house, boat, or car. First, you need to know its inherent value. If what you are restoring will not be of more value after it is restored, the project probably isn't worth pursuing. Second, you need to know what the object looked like originally. You would probably gather an old photo or drawing to inspire and help achieve your goal of restoration.

This is why the first two chapters of Genesis are so precious. Genesis 1 tells us the inherent value of marriage and family, and the second chapter describes what it originally looked like. Throughout this book, Genesis 1 and 2 will be our focus as we pursue the restoration of the original culture for marriage.

The Inherent Value of Marriage

Genesis 1:1 In the beginning God created the heavens and the earth.

Most of us are familiar with the creation account at the beginning of the Bible. Our Creator, God, begins His miraculous work, and, through the course of six days, creates an environment and culture for His children. On the first day, He creates light and separates it from the darkness. On the second, He creates a firmament between the waters. On the third, He creates dry land and the grasses, seeds, and trees on earth. On the fourth, He creates the sun, the moon, and all of the stars. On the fifth, He creates all of the fish of the sea and the birds of the air, and continues His creation into the sixth day, creating every land animal according to its kind.

As you read through the first six days of creation, you can't help but feel a momentum. It is important to read the account of creation from the perspective of a loving Father who sets the stage for what He intends to create later on the sixth day. The initial days of creation serve as the backdrop, the stage, and the props for the drama that is about to unfold—the climax of the story. Even the syntax is ordered: "God said, 'Let there be...' and there was, and God saw that it was good." However, when the sixth day arrives, there seems to be a shift. You can almost feel a dramatic pause; there is forethought and a heavenly conversation:

> Then God said, "Let us make man in our image, according to Our likeness; let them have dominion over the fish of the sea, over the birds of the air, and over the cattle, over all the earth and over every creeping thing that creeps on the earth." So God created man in His own image; in the image of God He created him; male and female He created them. Then God blessed them, and God said to them, "Be fruitful and multiply; fill the earth and subdue it; have dominion over the fish of the sea, over the birds of the air, and over every living thing that moves on the earth." (Genesis 1:26–28)

And so marriage and family enter the stage of world history.

You can feel the power and impact of the historical moment when the all-powerful creator, God, reveals Himself to His children and speaks to them for the first time. He sets them in a role of authority and gives them dominion over His culture.

"Be fruitful and multiply; fill the earth and subdue it" is rightfully named the Cultural Mandate. I believe this is the appropriate term; Adam and Eve are placed into the perfect culture, newly created by a loving Father and their mandate is to tend and care for the garden that they were given, rear children, and reproduce that culture across the face of the earth.

Have you ever considered why the Father creates the world unfilled and unsubdued? He did that for a very important reason: He wants His children to play a part in His creation; they are to absorb His culture and reproduce it. I believe the original mandate would have anticipated Adam and Eve's children expanding and growing their family's culture, taking seed from the tree of life and planting those seeds all over the face of the earth. They too, then, would eat of the tree, living forever in the presence of God, and reproduce the culture of their loving Father. This is the Father's mandate.

This is a very important truth for you to consider. When the Almighty God puts a plan in place and delivers a mandate, it never ends! Even if we walk away from that plan, operate in rebellion, or have no value for His mandate, His word isn't canceled. We don't have the authority or power to cancel His plan. When He sets something in place, it stays in place.

My wife, Amy, so eloquently wrote, "When Genesis chapter 3 happened, God's plan began to slip away from the memories of His children, but it *never* left His."

There is evidence of this when you consider the context of the whole book of Genesis. The historical organization is set forth in the beginning: "This is the history of the heavens and the earth when they were created, in the day the Lord God made the earth and the heavens," leading to the story of the Garden of Eden and the fall of man. After the beginning, there are nine other sections all introducing the generations of Adam, Noah, the sons of Noah, Shem, Terah, Ishmael, Isaac, Esau, and Jacob, which forms a basic outline of the book of Genesis. Each section in Genesis recounts how man responds to the command to fill the earth and to subdue it. The context of the whole book of Genesis, then, is a reiteration of the Father's persistent mandate. Here are some examples:

> Then God spoke to Noah, saying, "Go out of the Ark, you and your wife, and your sons and your sons' wives with you. Bring out with you every living thing of all flesh that is with you: birds and cattle and every creeping thing that creeps on the earth, so that they may abound on the earth, and *be fruitful and multiply* on the earth." (Genesis 8:15–17)

> "And I will make my covenant between me and you, and will *multiply* you exceedingly." Then Abram fell on his face, and God talked with him, saying: "As for me, behold, My covenant is with you, and you shall be a father of many nations.

> No longer shall your name be called Abram but your name shall be Abraham; for I've made you a father of many nations. I will make you exceedingly *fruitful*; and I will make nations of you and kings shall come from you." (Genesis 17:2–6)

> And God said to him, "Your name is Jacob; your name shall not be called Jacob anymore, but Israel shall be your name." So He called his name Israel. Also God said to him: "I am God Almighty. Be *fruitful and multiply*; a nation and accompanying nations shall proceed from you, and kings shall come from your body." (Genesis 35:10–11)

It makes sense that His mandate continues and persists through the generations, because the Lord never goes back on His word.

However, the Cultural Mandate becomes even more significant. Consider the importance of the Cultural Mandate in relation to God's special revelations to man recorded throughout the Bible. God's revelation to man is progressive, but it is not progressive in the sense that God's new revelation to man cancels what comes before it. Rather, God's new revelation builds upon His last. For example, it would be unwise to read the New Testament and ignore the Old Testament, the foundation upon which it was built. It would be equally foolish to read the Old Testament and consider it the final revelation. The same is true regarding the Cultural Mandate.

The Cultural Mandate is God's first special revelation to man. Therefore, God's instruction to "fill the earth and subdue it" is the foundation and centerpiece of all subsequent revelations to humankind! God does not go back on a word once spoken; He is constant. Therefore, it is of the utmost importance to keep the first, foundational word in mind when we listen to the many subsequent words God uses to address man.

Are you starting to understand how important your marriage and family is?

Marriage and family are the center point of the Cultural Mandate, which seems to be the center point of the sixth day of creation, which seems to be the climax of the creation week. The Cultural Mandate persists throughout the whole framework of Genesis. It is also the very center and foundation of all God's special revelations to man!

The first step in a family restoration project is to know the family's inherent value. The value and destiny of your marriage is beyond measure. It was and still is the center point of the Father's creative heart. You need to know that your marriage—and every marriage—is critical to the restoration and reproduction of the Father's original culture.

To minimize the importance and value of your marriage is to minimize the very heart of the Father!

What Marriage Originally Looked Like

The definition of culture can be described as, "the sum total ways of living built up by a group of human beings and transmitted from one generation to another." So, the second thing we need to know is what the Father's original culture looked like. If our marriage is critical to the restoration of the Father's culture, then we need to understand what we are aiming to restore.

Genesis 2 is one of my favorite chapters in the entire Bible. It is a snapshot in time of what the culture of Eden looks like before sin enters the world. The Father could have created anything He wanted, but Genesis 2 describes in detail what He chose to create for His children. As we dive deeper into the culture of Eden throughout this book, we will explore in much greater detail the events of Genesis chapters one, two, and three.

For this chapter, I have pulled out what I consider to be core cultural pieces found in Genesis 2. This is certainly not an exhaustive list, for I'm sure His culture and His goodness extends beyond what I can fathom. It is simply a list of cultural truths that could easily be found while studying chapter 2 verse by verse.

1. *Life* (verses 7, 9): The garden is not only the place where the Lord formed man and breathed into his nostrils the breath of life but also the environment and culture where they can grow and thrive. He plants in their midst the tree of life from which they can eat and live forever. Death, disease, and torment are never part of His culture.

2. *Boundaries* (verses 8–14): The Father makes it clear in His culture that Adam and Eve are not responsible for the entire world. They are responsible for what He gives them to tend and keep. Again, they are responsible for stewarding the culture in the garden and their children, who will reproduce that culture over the face of the earth. Boundaries are not created to restrict or to enslave us but to provide safety, security, and true freedom.

3. *Provision* (verses 9, 11, 12, 19): Perhaps, based on our experiences and disappointments, we may have mistakenly assumed that our God is a God of "just enough." However, that is not the case in His original culture. The culture of provision, described in Genesis 2, is extravagant. The garden is riddled with jewels and gemstones. It is described as having "good gold," and Adam and Eve enjoy "more than enough." God's creation gladly yields its fruit to humankind, and they are in want of nothing. God is also a God of pro-vision. He will breathe to life and bless humankind's creative vision, as they have dominion.

4. *Authority* (verses 16, 17, 19): There is a clear delineation of authority over the planet, from God creating man in His own image, to empowering all of humankind with dominion. God dictates to humankind what they can and cannot eat. Humankind is to operate within the authority and structure of the culture and will suffer the consequences if they choose not to.

5. *Truth* (verses 16, 17, Genesis 3:4): As stated previously, God's word is steadfast and unchanging. When He declares a mandate, a command, or a boundary, it persists and remains. His word is true. It makes perfect sense that the serpent questions the motives and truth of God's word when he says, "Has God indeed said, 'You shall not eat of every tree of the garden?'" and when he lies as he says, "You will not surely die." Adam and Eve quickly discover the absolute truth the moment they eat from the tree.

6. *Purpose and Task* (verses 15, 19, 20): The Father, in His loving wisdom, wants us to play a role in His creation. He creates the world unfilled and unsubdued and assigns the task of cultivating and tending the garden to Adam and Eve. They are to be stewards of the culture that He created and are to raise children to reproduce that culture. The Father's kingdom is exciting, and each of us individually, in our marriages and in our families, play a pivotal role in stewarding His culture.

7. *Covenant* (verses 18–24): I was raised in a culture that talked extensively about covenant, and my parents continue to teach this critical subject. My mother argued that covenant actually began, before creation, with the triunity. The Father demonstrates His unconditional and steadfast love to His children in the garden, and continues this demonstration of His heart by creating the first human covenant through marriage:

And the LORD God caused a deep sleep to fall on Adam, and he slept; and He took one of his ribs, and closed up the flesh in its place. Then the rib which the LORD God had taken from man He made into a woman, and He brought her to the man. And Adam said: "This is now bone of my bones and flesh of my flesh; she shall be called Woman, because she was taken out of Man." Therefore, a man shall leave his father and mother and be joined to his wife, and they shall become one flesh. (Genesis 2:21–24)

The word "rib" comes from the Hebrew word *tsela*, which is actually better translated to "side," rather than "rib." So, how much of his side does God actually remove? Perhaps even up to half of Adam. This makes more sense with the reference to bones *and* flesh.

This is a covenant surgery and ceremony, and its implications will be discussed in greater detail throughout this book. The Father's covenant of promises is a thread sewn throughout all of scripture.

8. *Freedom* (verse 25): "And they were both naked, the man and his wife, and were not ashamed." Within the loving boundaries of the Father, Adam and Eve operate in complete freedom, without the bondage of shame. In regard to marriage, this verse has no equal, because it represents the ultimate cultural aspiration for every marriage. This verse guides the direction for this entire book.

All of these eight cultural points are wonderful and should be the hallmark of every home, family, and marriage. However, despite how wonderful each of these is, they would not be available or sustainable without the last key cultural attribute.

9. *Relationship and Presence* (all of chapter 1 and 2, chapter 3:8): God creates us in the first place because He wants to be with us. He wants to hang out with His people! Our loving Father is a relational God, and from the very first day of creation, He never intends to be far off or removed from us. He actually walks with Adam and Eve in the cool of the day. The immensity of that truth is overwhelming! He even says it isn't good for man to be alone, so He creates an intimate relationship for Adam. Going through life alone is countercultural to his perfect plan.

Adam and Eve are completely satisfied in the Father's presence; they require nothing from each other for their worth or identity. It is truly an amazing culture.

Worth the Pursuit

For something to be restored, you need to know its *inherent value* and *what it originally looked like*. Hopefully, after reading this chapter, you realize that your family and marriage are valuable beyond measure, and are worth pursuing restoration. This doesn't mean simply fixing the problems—this means pursuing the full restoration of the Father's original heart and culture in your marriage. As you can see, it is a huge and glorious task.

This is supposed to be the end of the story. There isn't supposed to be sin and death. There isn't supposed to be any need for restoration. There isn't supposed to be any need for scripture. We are supposed to walk with the Father in the cool of the day and hear His words directly from His heart.

Unfortunately, we know the history of humankind doesn't end after two chapters. We know there's a chapter 3. We will explore the shift that takes place when we rebel from His culture and hide from His presence.

2

"The Way We Were"
Barbra Streisand, 1974

As we begin this chapter, I want to start by making an important point. In Genesis 1 and 2, the description of the Father's perfect creation for His children is normal and cultural. Everything that happens after Genesis 2 should be considered abnormal and countercultural.

As we pursue the culture of marriage and the greater depths of intimacy throughout this book, we will go into great detail about the events of Genesis 3. Too often, we view our fallen world and fallen relationships simply as the "new order" of things. However, when we consider the Father's original heart and what He created for us and for our marriages, we quickly realize that what happens in Genesis 3 is not the "new order;" it is the "out of order!"

Because marriages and families are exposed to the fallen culture and the pain that ensues, we can understand why our society pursues redefinition rather than restoration. If we change what marriage is or what it means, we hope that our own experiences will hurt less. We must refuse to redefine the Father's heart.

Because of the details to come, I will not emphasize the specific marital implications of humankind's rebellion in this chapter. However, I feel it is essential to contrast the culture found in the first two chapters of Genesis with the sorrow and heartbreak that occurs in Genesis 3.

Culture Lost

Genesis 3 is often referred to as "the curse" or "the fall of man." You are probably familiar with the account of the serpent tempting Adam and Eve to eat the fruit from the tree that they are commanded not to eat from. This rebellion sends them into a tailspin, and the loving culture the Father created is lost.

Following this event, the Father confronts the three offenders. I used to believe this confrontation was an angry father's chastisement toward disobedient children, and because He is so angry, He chooses to curse them. However, now that I have learned more about the Father's heart, I believe it is a heartbroken dissertation due to the shift He knows will happen. I believe the Father is drawing a picture of contrast between His original culture that He presents to them in Genesis 2 and what will be their new reality. First, He addresses the serpent:

> Because you have done this, you are cursed more than all cattle, and more than every beast of the field; on your belly you shall go, and you shall eat dust all the days of your life. And I will put enmity between you and the woman, and between your seed and her Seed; He shall bruise your head, and you shall bruise His heel. (Genesis 3:14, 15)

Satan is afforded residence on the earth; he is present but is of no effect. He has absolutely no authority or dominion, which was only given to humankind, and the only way he can receive authority or power is if humankind gives it to him. Unfortunately, this is exactly what happens. God makes it clear, that prior to his actions, Satan could have lived in relative anonymity, but from now on, he is marked. A culture of enmity between Satan and humankind has begun. From the very woman he deceives, a seed will come that ultimately cancels his newfound authority and the enmity that birthed it!

In Genesis 3:16, He says to the woman, "I will greatly multiply your sorrow and your conception; in pain you shall bring forth children; your desire shall for be your husband, and he shall rule over you."

The traditional interpretation of this verse makes the case that there is no pain in childbirth prior to sin, and after sin there will be pain in delivery. However, this doesn't adequately explain sorrow in conception. I believe this is not what scripture is telling us. I believe the Father is explaining to the woman that her children should have been born into the culture of Eden. Instead, her children will be born into a culture of enmity. That reality will result in incredible sorrow and pain, and, unfortunately, this is exactly what Eve feels when her firstborn son, Cain, kills her second son, Abel.

Remember, in the garden, Adam and Eve are completely satisfied in the presence of the Lord. The second portion of this passage is a warning: When separated from the Father's presence, Eve could mistakenly look to her husband to meet her needs, and as a result, her husband will rule over her.

> Then to Adam He said, "Because you heeded the voice of your wife, and have eaten from the tree of which I commanded you saying, 'you shall not eat of it': Cursed is the ground for your sake; in toil you shall eat of it all the days of your life. Both thorns and thistles it shall bring forth for you, And you shall eat the herb of the field. In the sweat of your face you shall eat bread till you return to the ground, for out of it you were taken; for dust you are, and to dust you shall return." (Genesis 3:17–19)

In the culture of Eden, nature gladly yields its fruit. Now, in the culture of enmity, creation itself is subject to bondage and disorder. I don't believe thorns and thistles were created in Genesis 3. I believe they were a disorderly expression of a fallen creation, and they did not belong in the fields. Instead of having dominion, humankind will toil with creation. Instead of the culture of Eden, where they were meant to eat from the tree of life and live forever, they will now experience death.

Simply put, the lovely and glorious culture that they experienced in the first chapter has shifted:

1. Instead of a culture of life, they now have a culture of *death*.

2. Instead of a culture with loving boundaries where they will find freedom, safety and security, they will now operate in *anxiety*.

3. Instead of a culture of provision, they will now operate in *lack*, under the sweat of their brow.

4. Instead of a culture of authority, they will operate in *rebellion*.

5. Instead of a culture of truth, they are exposed to the *counterfeit*. Satan is not a creator. Scripture refers to him as the father of lies, so he can only bring forth distortion and lies.

6. Instead of the culture of purpose and task, where they receive direction from the Father, they are now confused and *burdened*.

7. Instead of the culture of covenant, which means "all that I have is yours and all that you have mine," they are consumed by *self*.

8. Instead of a culture of freedom, they live in a culture of *bondage*.

9. The culture of Eden is established on the relationship with and the presence of the Father. Even after the Father knows of their sin, He goes to them. However, because of their *shame*, they go into *hiding*, choosing to separate from His culture and His presence, which results in the loss of the culture.

A Father's Pursuit

His children, made in His image, are lost, along with the culture provided to them. His children, in every sense, are orphans.

All we have to do is turn on the news at night to see that we are still affected by a culture of enmity. We get angry and frustrated at the behavior of those in our culture; however, we need to understand that the problems we see in society aren't really problems, they are the symptoms of an orphan world, whose children live in pain from separation from their Father and loss of identity.

Let's be clear, the loving character of our Father never changes. He, in His sovereignty, gives us free will. He, like any good father, is heartbroken by our choices. But be assured of this, He never stops pursuing a relationship with us!

The Old Testament is really a story of a father, separated from his children, who is trying to reconnect with them any way he can. Story after story depicts the Father reaching out to His children...only to be rejected time and time again. For example, in the account of Moses on Mount Sinai, Moses experiences a measure of the Father's presence. The Lord tells Moses to give the people an invitation to join Him on the mountain. Upon hearing the invitation, the people are afraid and reject the offer. The Bible says, "They stood far off." All the tabernacles, offerings, arks and veils could not satisfy the longing of the Father's heart for His children. There is only one answer, only one way: the seed.

According to Galatians 4:4,5, "When the fullness of the time had come, God sent forth His son, born of a woman, born under the law, to redeem those who were under the law, that we might receive the adoption as sons."

I believe the "fullness of time" means the Father simply couldn't wait any longer. Jesus not only came to earth on a salvation mission but also on a restoration mission!

The Seed

Let's explore the fullness of what Jesus accomplished on the cross and the exciting times in which we currently live by moving from Genesis 3 to Acts 3.

This is the story of a lame man well known by the entire community, who is discovered by Peter and John when they go to pray. The lame man asks for money, and Peter and John explain that, although they have no money to give, they can offer him something of much greater worth: healing and restoration. This man is so exuberant after his healing that he runs and leaps, creating a scene. A crowd gathers and Peter delivers one of the most powerful, spontaneous, Holy Spirit–inspired messages while the healed man clings to their sides.

> Men of Israel, why do you marvel at this? Or why look so intently at us, as though by our own power or godliness we had made this man walk? The God of Abraham, Isaac, and Jacob, the God of our fathers, glorified His Servant Jesus, whom you delivered up and denied in the presence of Pilate, when he was determined to let Him go. But you denied the Holy One and the Just, and asked for a murderer to be granted to you, and killed the Prince of life, whom God raised from the dead, of which we are witnesses. And His name, through faith in His name, has made this man strong, whom you see and know. Yes, the faith which comes through Him has given him this *perfect soundness* in the presence of you all. Yet now, brethren, I know that you did it in ignorance, as did also your rulers. But those things which God foretold by the mouth of all His prophets, that the Christ would suffer, He has thus fulfilled. Repent therefore and be converted, that your sins may be blotted out, so that times of *refreshing may come from the presence of the Lord*, and that

He may send Jesus Christ, who was preached to you before, whom heaven must receive until the *times of restoration of all things*, which God has spoken by the mouth of all His holy prophets since the world began. For Moses truly said to the fathers, 'The LORD your God will raise up for you a Prophet like me from your brethren. Him you shall hear in all things, whatever He says to you. And it shall be that every soul who will not hear that Prophet shall be utterly destroyed from among the people." Yes, and all the prophets, from Samuel and those who follow, as many as have spoken, have also foretold *these days*. You are sons of the prophets, and of the covenant which God made with our fathers, saying to Abraham, "And in your seed all the *families* of the earth shall be blessed." (Acts 3:12–25)

    Many may try to push this passage off as the second coming of Jesus, but Peter is making the claim that all the Prophets of old were speaking of *these days*! He asks the crowd why they are marveling over this man's expected restoration. Peter understands that this miracle is simply one expected manifestation of the work of Jesus on the cross and His resurrection.
    In addition to healing, the crowd should expect restored refreshment in the presence of the Lord. Remember, prior to Jesus, there was a veil between humankind and His refreshing presence. Now, the veil is torn in two, and His presence is accessible to all!

Finally, Peter claims that all the families of the earth will be blessed. Why is that so important? Because families are central to His original plan! He is saying that they—we—are living in the time of restoration of *all* things! Bodies restored, presence restored, families restored, does this sound familiar?

Culture Restored

You see, Jesus puts the culture of Eden back into play! What is lost, Jesus restores! The Bible doesn't say that Jesus came to seek and save the lost. Rather, it says, "Jesus came to seek and save *that which* was lost!" (Matthew 18:11)

Jesus restores the culture of *life, truth,* and *presence*:

> Jesus said to him, "I am the way, the truth, and the life. No one comes to the Father except through Me." (John 14:6)

Jesus restores the culture of *boundaries*:

> Then Jesus answered and said to them, "Most assuredly, I say to you, the Son can do nothing of Himself, but what He sees the Father do; for whatever He does, the Son also does in like manner." (John 5:19)

Jesus restores the culture of *provision*:

> But even now I know that whatever You ask of God, God will give You. (John 11:22)

> And my God will supply all your needs according to His riches in glory in Christ Jesus. (Philippians 4:19)

Jesus restores the culture of *authority*:

> And Jesus came and spoke to them, saying, "All authority has been given to Me in heaven and on earth." (Matthew 28:18)

Jesus restores the culture of *purpose* and *task*:

> Go therefore and make disciples of all the nations, baptizing them in the name of the Father and of the Son and of the Holy Spirit, teaching them to observe all things that I have commanded you; and lo, I am with you always, even to the end of the age. (Matthew 28:19, 20)

> Make you complete in every good work to do His will, working in you what is well pleasing in His sight, through Jesus Christ. (Hebrews 13:21)

Jesus restores the culture of the *covenant*:

> For this is My blood of the new covenant, which is shed for many for the remission of sins. (Matthew 26:28)

Jesus restores the culture of *freedom*:

> It is for freedom that Christ has set us free. Stand firm, then, and do not let yourselves be burdened again by a yoke of slavery. (Galatians 5:1 New International Version)

Jesus is the family restoration project. This extends not only to our relationship with the Father but also to our individual family relationships. When Jesus is nailed to the cross, our enmity is removed. Our children are no longer born into a culture of enmity!

Birth Pangs

Remember, this is the restoration of *all* things. It extends beyond relationships into all of creation.

> For I consider that the sufferings of this present time are not worthy to be compared with the glory which shall be revealed in us. For the earnest expectation of the creation eagerly waits for the revealing of the sons of God. For the creation was subjected to futility, not willingly,

but because of Him who subjected it in hope; because the creation itself also will be delivered from the *bondage* of corruption into the glorious liberty of the children of God. For we know that the whole creation groans and labors with birth pangs together until *now*. (Romans 8:18–22)

Even creation is eagerly waiting for the children of God to understand the times in which we live, because the time is *now*! It has been the time ever since Jesus walks out of the grave. We just need to realize and embrace the power and fullness of Jesus's blood that lives in us now.

Jesus will come back again; however, He is not coming back as the savior. He has already done that. He will come back as a bridegroom, with fire in his eyes for his bride! Until then, we, as God's children, have work to do. He doesn't want us to be a tired and tattered bride, just holding on until He returns. No, He wants us to be pure, without spots or wrinkles, fulfilling our destiny for which we were created.

We live in very exciting times, and we should expect to see the manifestation of His blood and resurrection in *these days*. This means that the culture we loved and learned about in Genesis 1 and 2 is back in play! This means we should expect to see our marriages and families restored. Restoration is possible because it is purchased for us with the blood of Jesus. This means the loving Father never stops pursuing you, and His heart toward you never changes. Because of Jesus, His children have easy access to the loving presence and relationship with the Father.

However, even in the culture of Eden, we still have free will. We, as His children, yes, even Christian children, have been orphans a long time. For some, the notion of entering into a relationship with the Father is intimidating. Some feel it is unnecessary—that a relationship with Jesus is enough. But full restoration can only happen through the healing of our identity, and our identity can only be found in the Father. It is critical to address the orphan spirit in each of us. It needs to be healed first in order for healing to occur in every marriage and family.

In the next chapter, we will learn how to identify—and become free from—the orphan spirit and discover how that freedom will propel you to pursue greater depths of intimacy in your marriage.

3

"I Still Haven't Found What I'm Looking For"

U2, 1987

The first two chapters of this book set a foundation for the journey into the greater depths of marriage. In order to pursue full restoration, you need to know that your marriage is valuable; you need to know what marriage originally looked like; and you need to understand the culture the Father intends for humankind. It is also essential to know that His marriage culture is restorable. He is a God of restoration and He sent His Son on a restoration mission. His mission is fully accomplished on the cross and, because of His resurrection, we live in "the times of restoration of all things."

If it is true that the culture of Eden is once again available to us and our Father has made a way back into a relationship and presence with us, then we need to have a full revelation of who we are and what it means to be His children.

Declaring a Father

> He was in the world, and the world was made through Him, and the world did not know Him. He came to his own, and His own did not receive Him. But as many as received Him, to them He gave the *right to become children of God,* to those who believe in His name; who were born not of blood, nor of the will of the flesh, nor of the will of man, but of God. And the Word became flesh and dwelt among us, and we beheld His glory, the glory as of the only begotten of the Father, full of grace and truth...For the law was given through Moses, but grace and truth came through Jesus Christ. No one has seen God at any time. The only begotten Son, who is in the bosom of the Father, *He has declared Him.* (John 1:10–14, 17–18)

Jesus came to declare the Father to an orphaned world. After thousands of years of separation from the Father's heart and culture, Jesus came to be a spotless and pure representation of Him.

Jesus says he is the "Door" (John 10:9). My question is, the door to what? He says, "I am the Way." The way to what? "I am the way and the truth and the life, no one comes to the *Father* but by me" (John 14:6). He is the only way to the Father and His loving heart. The Father revealed to me that the church today is "dancing at the door." We celebrate the life and sacrifice of Jesus, and rightfully so. In my opinion, though, we may have missed the very heart of His mission. He saved us from our sins, and brought us everlasting life—that is secure and sure. However, Jesus wants to usher us through the door into His Father's kingdom where there is life, restoration, and, perhaps most importantly, His original culture.

You see, Jesus didn't come to replace the Father. He came to restore our place in the Father!

John 1:12 says, "As many as received Him, to them He gave the right to become children of God." This also means that those who have received Him as savior have the right to stay orphans! It is easy to see the effect of this *orphan spirit* when on display "in the world." However, it is sobering to realize that the orphan spirit is alive and well in Christian homes and churches as well.

The Pivot

This orphan spirit has been around since Genesis 3, introduced by the first orphan, Satan. His sinister plan never changes. His strategy is to keep us from the loving heart of the Father, but what does this have to do with marriage and family? The orphan spirit is ominous, and when we are separated from the Father's voice and His loving kingdom and culture, it will infect every one of our relationships.

Remember once again, Adam and Eve are completely satisfied in the presence of a loving Father before the fall. When we are separated from that presence, we will look to others to meet our needs. In contrast, when we are sons and daughters of Him, we look to serve others.

The Father gave me the picture that orphans pivot; they plant their foot and spin around in every direction to see who can meet their needs. Whereas sons and daughters of God simply listen to the Father's voice and run where He instructs.

Orphans hear many voices. This can often feel confusing and lead to anxiety. They hear a lot of static. Sons and daughters hear only one voice.

Orphans strive for praise and approval and easily feel rejected. Sons and daughters are accepted in the Father's love and feel affirmed.

Orphans are consumed by competition and rivalry. Sons and daughters rejoice in others' blessings.

Orphans can only see God as master and commander. Sons and daughters see Him as a loving father.

Orphan Circles

So, let's see how this orphan spirit affects our marriages, families, relationships, and our society. Here is Mr. Christian orphan. He has accepted Christ and loves Him as Lord and Savior. He has not, however, understood that Jesus is the Door to the Father's kingdom and is uncomfortable with the

love of the Father. Because he is not satisfied in the presence of the Father, he looks to others to meet his needs. He hopes someone else can cover the pain of his orphan heart. One day, he sees a beautiful woman and begins a relationship with her. This relationship meets his need for worth and identity, and they decide to get married.

Their marriage is based on meeting their needs and trying to conceal their orphan spirit. They quickly realize they are unwilling and unable to meet the needs of their spouse, and in return, their needs are also not being met. Trying to live up to expectations becomes a heavy weight that leads to rejection and  disappointment when they fall short. But there is still hope for this Christian couple.

They have children. Raising a family brings a renewed sense of unity to their marriage, and for a 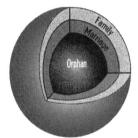 time, being parents and starting a family gives them a sense of worth and accomplishment and creates another layer of covering over their orphan heart. Their children are raised with a sense that they should try to meet their parent's needs. The parents quickly find their children are unable to meet those needs, which weighs on the children as they try to live up to their parents' expectations. They feel rejected and disappointed when they can't. But there is still hope for this Christian family.

This family belongs to a church, and they hope to rely on their pastors to meet their needs. Churches are created to meet the needs of the lost, the poor, the sick, the widows, and the orphans. Pastors are made to equip the saints for that work but quickly find they are unable to meet all the needs of their orphan members. Pastors feel a heavy weight placed upon 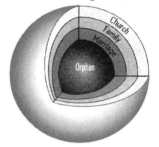 them, trying to run an "orphanage" and live up to their congregation's expectations, and they feel rejection and disappointment when they can't meet or exceed them. When their needs are not met, orphans often 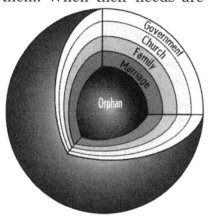 leave to find another orphanage. But there is still hope.

Orphans have the government. The government, which is over $20 trillion in debt, picks up causes that don't belong to them. The church has accused the government of "overreaching," but in reality the government needs to take over the care of the poor, the sick, the widows, and the orphans. This creates a domino effect where:

The government has picked up something that doesn't belong to them...

Because churches have picked up something that doesn't belong to them...

Because children have picked up something that doesn't belong to them...

Because spouses have picked up something that doesn't belong to them...

All because we are *orphans!*

The orphan spirit and our separation from the Father affect all aspects of relationships and society. When trying to bring about healing and restoration, we are often guilty of chasing the symptoms rather than discovering the disease or the root cause of the problem.

The root cause is *identity*. Which leads me to the most critical question: Who are you?

Many would answer this question with identifying answers such as their name, occupation, or family situation. Some may try to sound spiritual and say, "I am Christian." However, saying you are a Christian is an allegiance, not an identity. It is vital, as we pursue restoration, that you are able to answer this question: Who are you?

Here's the answer: *You are a loved son or daughter of the most high God!*

Most Christians, if asked, will confidently say that God loves them. But then I will ask you: Do you see that as your identity? Do you truly see yourself as royalty, an actual son or daughter of the most high God?

You cannot move forward until you are confident in your position or identity. Everything we do needs to be done from a place of secure identity. Without value for your identity, you will be tempted to only pursue purpose or power in His kingdom. However, if you attempt to find purpose or to wield power as an orphan, you will only cause pain for yourself and others. You need to find *position* first, then purpose, and then power.

A Loving Father

The problem is, if we are being honest, many are uncomfortable with the notion that God is a loving father. There is no way to separate your feelings for God as a father from your feelings for your natural mother and father. Your mom and dad shape your understanding and create a paradigm for what a father means.

I understand that many people's experience with their father has not been a positive one. But some may have had an experience like I had, one where the mother and father demonstrate the Father's love extremely well, which allows me to read and study about the Father and readily accept His love for me.

On the other hand, there may be some who never had a father or mother figure. Perhaps one of your parents was absent. Because of this, it is quite possible that you see the Father as erratic and unreliable.

Alternatively, you may have had a present father and mother, but your relationship with them was destructive. Perhaps your parents were angry and abusive or they deeply hurt you. If this is your experience, you may even hate the word "father," and want nothing to do with a heavenly one.

Despite all of these different backgrounds and experiences, we need to turn to the One—the only One—who knows the Father perfectly: Jesus. He came to declare His Father to each and everyone of us. Jesus came to change the way we think about the Father, and then, through His blood, usher us back into His presence.

You see, Jesus said, "He only does what He sees the Father do" (John 5:19). So, when Jesus restores the woman caught in the act of adultery, opens blind eyes, touches and heals the leper, casts out demons, and raises the dead, He is declaring the Father! When He tells stories about the kingdom of heaven, He isn't just reciting a tale to help us with life. He is sharing with us what the Father and His kingdom are like. When He starts a story with "The kingdom of heaven is like…" it isn't to tell us what to do, but to tell us who He is.

A Partying Mood

I believe the story of the prodigal son (Luke 15) isn't about the son at all; it's about the father, who sees his son far off and runs to him. This is the same son who squanders his inheritance and concludes that he will be better off as a slave in his father's house. However, when the father greets his son upon his return, he wants nothing to do with his son becoming a slave. Rather, he puts a ring on his son's finger, a cloak on his back, and he kills the fatted calf and throws him a party. Do you see? The father exclaims, "My son was lost and now is found, he was dead but now he is alive!" Jesus tells us this parable to reveal something about His Father. The Father isn't angry and disappointed when his wayward son returns home, he is in a partying mood!

The Father desires us to have an intimate father-son or father-daughter relationship with Him. He is not a figurative father, and we are not His metaphorical children. He created us, gave us life, and released us to our destiny. We are His joy and the apples of His eye, and He is our Daddy.

> For you did not receive the spirit of bondage again to fear, but you received the Spirit of adoption by whom we cry out, "Abba, Father." The Spirit Himself bears witness with our spirit that we are children of God, and if children, then heirs—heirs of God and joint heirs with Christ, if indeed we suffer with Him, that we may also be glorified together. (Rom. 8:15–17)

The word "Abba" is the casual, familiar word a young Hebrew child calls his father. It is very much the equivalent of the word "daddy" or "papa." The most literal interpretation is "da-da." Remember, spiritual bondage is introduced into the world because of sin, and our awareness of sin and shame separates us from our loving Father. This passage in Romans makes the incredible assertion that the spirit of bondage is displaced by the spirit of adoption! The spirit of adoption is so powerful and restoring. When we receive the spirit of adoption, we are given the right to once again be called children. There should be a manifestation within us that cries out, "Daddy!" Paul feels this is so important he repeats this again:

> Even so we, when we were children, were in bondage under the elements of the world. But when the fullness of the time had come, God sent forth His Son, born of a woman, born under the law, to redeem those who were under the law, that we might receive the adoption as sons. And because you are sons, God has sent forth the Spirit of His Son into your hearts, crying out, "Abba, Father!" Therefore you are no longer a slave but a son, and if a son, then an heir of God through Christ. (Galatians 4:3–7)

This passage refers to the same manifestation that wells up within us and cries out, "Abba, Daddy." This is the same invitation of adoption. However, this passage refers to it as the "spirit of His Son." The spirit of adoption is the heartbeat of the mission of Jesus.

The spirit of His Son is to declare the Father!

The Bible says that Jesus endured the cross for the joy that was set before Him. Many have their opinion as to what that joy is. I believe that Jesus endures the cross for His Father, because He is bringing the kids back!

Because of His sacrifice, the price that He pays, we need to take this issue of sonship and identity seriously.

The Bible is a different book when you read it as a son rather than a slave. Remember, the phrase "the kingdom of heaven is like..." is our cue that this is about Papa.

> Again, the kingdom of heaven is like treasure hidden in the field, and for the joy over it he goes and sells all that he has and buys that field. Again, the kingdom of heaven is like a merchant seeking beautiful pearls, who, when he had found one pearl of great price, went and sold all that he had and bought it. (Matthew 13:44, 45)

I always thought this verse meant that we need to sell all that we have to Jesus to purchase all that He is. But this is about Papa; Jesus is telling us about His Father. From this perspective, these verses are transformational. Jesus explains to us that *we* are the treasure hidden in the field, and *we* are the pearl of great price! The Father emptied heaven to come and get us. He gave all that He had in order to bring His children back!

Displaced by His Love

The orphan spirit is a different kind of spirit. It cannot simply be "cast out." It must be displaced. We can only displace the orphan spirit by entering back into a relationship with the Father and receiving the fullness of His love.

First, we must pursue identity. We need to be able to look into the mirror and confidently say, "I am a loved son or daughter of the most high God."

Second, we must know that the Father is safe and loving. We may need to pursue healing from any current or childhood trauma or pain that will hinder our ability to wholeheartedly receive the Father's love. Then, we must simply receive, and He so freely gives His love. Through the sacrifice of his Son, we can once again enter into His presence and experience His love.

I highly recommend calling Him "Daddy." I know to some of you this may sound irreverent, and I understand this, but this isn't my idea—this is His idea. It would be silly if I came home from work and my children ran out to greet me, and in a slightly British accent said, "Greetings father, how art thou?" I wouldn't like this at all as their father. I would much prefer them to wrap their arms around my neck and cry out, "Daddy!" Well, according to Romans and Galatians, this is exactly what our Father in heaven wants us to do as well. It may sound awkward at first, but give it a try. Receive the spirit of adoption and allow it to well up within you so that you can't help but cry out, "Abba, Daddy, Papa!"

Receiving our rightful identity as sons and daughters will require stewardship. The enemy is crafty and relentless, and just as he does in the Garden of Eden, he will repeatedly confront you and challenge your identity. You need to be aware and ready. The first Adam was unsuccessful in stewarding and protecting his identity. However, the second Adam, when confronted in the wilderness and challenged by the enemy, stood firm and resisted His temptation. The Father affirmed His Son and said, "This is my beloved Son, in whom I am well pleased" (Matthew 3:17). As incredible as it sounds, He speaks the same about us today!

We will learn that displacing the orphan spirit within each of us is absolutely essential in our marriages.

As we have laid the foundation for marriage in these first three chapters, I have made reference to pursuing greater depths of intimacy, and ultimately reaching what I call "the ultimate." Starting with the next chapter, we will begin this journey. With the culture of Eden back in play, we will examine what the Father created marriage for at the beginning of time.

There are four key words of increasing depth. These four words reflect the original culture of marriage, and fittingly, are found in the first two chapters of Genesis. They will give us a starting point on the path toward full restoration and will help us progress all the way to the ultimate culture of marriage. Not surprisingly, these four words will also reflect the culture of Heaven itself.

Following each of these words will be a chapter addressing a particular aspect of the orphan spirit that may seek to undermine the Father's culture and keep you and your spouse from progressing to greater depths of intimacy.

4

"Happy Together"
The Turtles, 1967

It is fitting that the first of the four words that describe how the marriage culture of Eden reflects the culture of heaven is found in the very first chapter of the Bible.

> Then God said, "Let Us make man in Our image, according to Our likeness; let *them* have dominion over the fish of the sea, over the birds of the air, and over the cattle, over all the earth and over every creeping thing that creeps on the earth." So God created man in His own image; in the image of God He created him; male and female He created *them*. Then God blessed *them*, and God said to *them*, "Be fruitful and multiply; fill the earth and subdue it; have dominion over the fish of the sea, over the birds

of the air, and over every living thing that moves on the earth." (Genesis 1:26–28)

Them

The Father gives the culture He created, and, more specifically, His original plan for marriage and family to both of *them*, Adam *and* Eve. The Father is very specific about the culture He wished to create, and His plan is not conducive to Adam being alone. In fact, of all of the things the Father creates, there is only one thing He proclaims to be "not good." He proclaims, "It is not good that man should be alone." (Genesis 2:18)

Our Almighty Creator is relational. I believe He infuses His heart into His creation. He sees that it is not good for man to be alone, so He creates a culture where they are co-missioned. It is from this culture that they are not able to do alone what needs to be done together. His original mission is given to *them*.

The First Great Co-mission

As mentioned earlier in this book, Genesis 1:28 is called the Cultural Mandate; sometimes I like to call it the *first great co-mission*. There is no greater demonstration on earth of His commissioning heart than marriage. Family, and more specifically marriage, is the subject of the first great co-mission: "Be fruitful and multiply; fill the earth and subdue it."

The culture of the Father created in the garden is one of dependence; to complete the mission, Adam and Eve need to operate in complete dependence on God and one another.

We are created, since the beginning of time, to carry a co-mission in, and through, our marriage. This is not a trivial notion. This speaks very strongly to the incredible inherent value of marriage! The foundational aspect of marriage and all of societal culture begins in the garden when the first great co-mission is given to *them*.

If you are single and reading this book, please understand that the Father has a purpose and mission for you that is uniquely yours in your singlehood. Only you can accomplish this mission. Too often, singles feel like their life doesn't really begin until they are co-missioned in marriage. Remember, Genesis doesn't say it is not good for man to be *single*, but rather, it says *alone*. Also, it is important to remember that, when you are single, you are still living in the context of a family. Your nuclear family is also co-missioned, and I recommend that you discover the fullness of that commission and lean into it. However, you will discover that, when you do become married, there will be new things for you to do in His kingdom. It will be a co-mission that can only be done together as husband and wife.

The Second Great Co-mission

Although the marriage co-mission is unique in its importance and foundation, I believe the notion of being commissioned is not unique to marriage. All throughout our lives, whether married or single, young or old, male or female, we are given various missions from our Father for His kingdom. As stated before, it is essential that we hear the Father's voice. We should do all—and only—what He asks of us.

Invariably, we will need support from others and we will need to be the support for others. There will be particular "missions" where we will be co-missioned with others, and the task will be accomplished only through partnership and unity. There are purposes for His kingdom that can only manifest if done together. This is the way the Father created it to be. If you prefer to live life as a solitary being, not requiring help from anyone, then you are living countercultural to the Father's original intention. If you have problems getting along with other people, you need to get over it! He created us as relational beings, and there are things for His kingdom that are unlocked when His children learn to operate in unity and interdependency.

The body of Christ, His church, is the recipient of the "second great co-mission."

> And Jesus came and spoke to them, saying, "All authority has been given to Me in heaven and on earth. Go therefore and make disciples of all nations, baptizing them in the name of the

Father and of the Son and of the Holy Spirit, teaching them to observe all things that I have commanded you; and lo, I am with you always, even to the end of the age." (Matthew 28:18)

I believe the first great co-mission is for family and marriage to set and reproduce the culture. The second great co-mission is for the church to equip the saints to do the work in the culture. The Bible says the church is created :

> ...for the equipping of the saints for the work of ministry, for the edifying of the body of Christ, till all come to the unity of the faith and of the knowledge of the Son of God, to a perfect man, to the measure of the stature of the fullness of Christ; that we should no longer be children, tossed to and fro and carried about with every wind of doctrine, by the trickery of men, in the cunning craftiness of deceitful plotting, but, speaking the truth in love, may grow up in all things into Him who is the head-Christ-from whom the whole body, joined and knit together by what every joint supplies, according to the effective working by which every part does its share, causes growth of the body for the edifying of itself in love. (Ephesians 4:12–16)

We are co-missioned with Christ and co-missioned with each other, until all have come together under the unity of faith and the knowledge of the Son of God. Once again, this work can only be done together.

Unity of Purpose

It is the ministry of the Holy Spirit to create in us the spirit of unity. Unity is the desire and value of working together to accomplish the mission. Through the power of the Holy Spirit we will grow and mature in the spirit of unity.

> I, therefore, the prisoner of the Lord, beseech you to walk worthy of the *calling with which you were called*, with all lowliness and gentleness, with longsuffering, bearing with one another in love, endeavoring to keep the *unity of the Spirit* in the bond of peace. (Ephesians 4:1–3)

The hallmark of commissioning is the *unity of purpose*. Pursuing unity is a calling to every marriage and is fundamental to the success of carrying out the first great co-mission. It is also a call to the church and is foundational to the success of carrying out the second great co-mission.

Everyone desires unity in his or her marriage, but unity is not unique to marriage. It is essential that we learn the spirit of unity before we get married.

It is valuable to learn what it means to be unified in childhood, to put others' needs in front of our own for the purposes to which we are commissioned. When we realize God brings other people into our lives to help us and facilitate His purposes, we will place greater value on unity. When this value becomes part of who we are, our calling and commission in marriage becomes much more intuitive.

To pursue unity in your marriage, you need to go back to the culture of the garden. The first great co-mission is foundational to every marriage; "Be fruitful, multiply; fill the earth and subdue it" is still the clarion call of marriage and culture across the face of the earth. We are called to something great! We are given a culture that is to be reproduced, multiplied, and injected into the earth as the culture for all society.

The key is to know why you are commissioned and what you are commissioned for. This is only found in the Father's voice, the Author of all things.

Run

As previously explained, sons and daughters hear only one voice, whereas orphans hear many. Remember, orphans pivot. They spin around looking for someone to meet their needs. When we are single, it is important to hear the Father's voice clearly, because when we hear the Father's voice, we can run with confidence in our mission. We simply run in the direction He tells us to run. There may come a day during our run when the Holy Spirit gently turns our head to the side to see if someone is running with us. I believe this is the ideal way to find our spouse. At that moment, the Holy Spirit will ask you if you are willing to be co-missioned.

However, for the vast majority of us, this is not the way we select our spouse. If we are honest, most of us select our spouse because they met our needs. The orphan spirit is tricky. The void in us likes what marriage offers us, but we don't always like the idea of being interdependent with another person. We love the idea of companionship and living a life together, but we often fail to see or appreciate the inherent value of the co-mission. So often, marriages consist of two people desperately trying to remain independent—to run separately—who are surprised when their marriage is, in a word, dis-unified.

Eating from His Table

My wife and I always felt a strong commissioning to have a large family. In fact, my wife felt a call to be a wife and mother at a very young age. We met when she was in nursing school. One day, her instructor asked the class to write down where they envisioned their life to be in five years. Amy wrote: Married, retired from nursing, at home raising children! (I don't think this is what the instructor had in mind.)

When we went through premarital counseling in our church where we met, they asked us "why" we wanted to have children. When we gave a detailed answer, they were surprised and said it was the first time, in all of their counseling experience, that a couple was able to confidently articulate why they wanted to have children when initially asked. We understood our co-mission.

However, as we began to have more and more children, ultimately having eight, I felt my orphan spirit rise up in protest. I also felt I had a self-mission. I envisioned a speaking ministry and could not reconcile that ever happening with a full-time medical practice and eight children. I didn't feel called to "just" be a husband and father. I began to experience bitterness and disunity toward my wife, as she was living her dream and I felt mine slipping away. The orphan spirit is tricky; it makes you feel entitled, offended, and misunderstood. I looked to my wife for my worth and my identity, yet I felt she had no interest to meet those needs.

Then, everything started to shift in our home. My wife had a radical experience in the Father's love, and the obvious, glorious change in her transformed the entire atmosphere and culture in our home. The orphan spirit was displaced out of our home through the outrageous love of our Daddy, God.

I was a high functioning orphan. Like any good orphan, I felt that performing hard for the Lord meant I would be loved more. Prior to my own love encounters with the Father, I was running hard. I loved Jesus, I would do anything for Him, and I was doing plenty.

When I walked around our acreage in rural Minnesota, I heard Him speak to me as a father speaks to his son. He was loving and gentle and convinced me that He loved me no matter what I did or didn't do. He told me He didn't want me to *do*, He wanted me to *be*. He began to strip away all my performance mentality and selfish ambition. I remember stopping and saying,

"Daddy, as long as I'm eating from Your table, I'm satisfied." If that meant I was to "just" be a husband and father, then I would be content.

Shortly thereafter, I did something very brave. I sat down with a blank sheet of paper and asked my Papa what He wanted me to do. I was busy doing a lot of things, but now I was a son, so I wanted to hear His voice. The list He gave me was very short, and the first thing he told me was to "go home and play board games with your kids," so I did.

All of the other things we were doing had to go away and we "hunkered down" and just "did family." Not surprisingly, He began to speak to me about my family. I would frequently wake up during the night with "downloads" from heaven about family. We were satisfied and content with the bread we were being fed.

Eventually, He told us that what was given to us as bread needed to be sown as seed. Soon, my speaking ministry began. It wasn't my message, it was His message. You see, the desire and call on my life was real, but He wouldn't send me as an orphan. It needed to be His voice and His timing and a co-mission with my wife and family. From a place of identity, we could then move in unity of purpose. First position, then purpose, and then power.

Entry-Level

Unity isn't a unique value to marriage—it is the entry-level step to examining the greater depths of marriage. Sometimes, to bring healing and restoration to our marriages, we have to go back to the beginning. It is so important that we have value for the Father's original plan for our marriage. It is quite possible that you have never considered that you are co-missioned with your spouse, and perhaps you have never considered that there are missions you are called to do together that cannot be done alone.

It may be time to come before the Holy Spirit and, to once again or for the first time, ask Him why you are commissioned and why you are married. It is never too late! The Holy Spirit is not fragile, and He is not limited to time. He is a God of restoration.

Reminisce with your spouse about how you met, pull out your marriage photo album, and ask the Holy Spirit to bring restoration to the original call and co-mission in your marriage. The Father will speak to you about your unique purpose together.

Consider doing something very brave. Sit down with a blank sheet of paper and ask the Father what He wants you to do. Ask Him what is *and* what is not yours to carry.

This in turn, will bring a new, refreshing energy and excitement to your marriage. Most importantly, it will reignite your unity of purpose.

Even though unity is the entry-level step, it can also be the last straw in some marriages. Lack of unity can destroy any relationship. This is certainly the case in friendships, business relationships, and definitely in the church. How much more can lack of unity cripple marriages?

Remember, disunity isn't a problem; it is a symptom. The problem is always identity. The solution is always the Father's love.

The next chapter will examine the independent spirit. The independent spirit is a subcategory of the orphan spirit. It turns what is intended to be a co-mission into a self-mission, and this has had a devastating effect on marriages, unity, and the culture of marriage all over the world.

5

"How Am I Supposed to Live Without You"

Michael Bolton, 1990

Now that I know I am a loved son of the most high God, I have more courage to ask the Father difficult questions. I fully understand that He's not obliged to answer all of my questions, but the crazy part is, sometimes He does.

One day, as I was riding my lawn mower, I felt a mix of awe, wonderment, and outright frustration. I was reading *The Dancing Hand of God* by James Maloney, in which he describes an event in India. He tells the story of a man, who, because of a congenital disorder, has no arm. The Lord uses an unsuspecting vessel on James Maloney's team to pray for this man, and miraculously, his arm begins to grow right in front of their eyes! Needless to say, I was floored. I was so appreciative of our loving, compassionate Father, but also a little frustrated because this sort of thing doesn't seem to happen here in the United States. Why don't we regularly see these kinds of miracles in the United States?

Now, I fully understand that things are shifting as the American church presses toward these manifestations, but it seems to me that so many of these stories take place in Argentina, India, or Africa. I asked the Lord, while riding my lawn mower, why that is the case. Why, in these dark places, do the craziest miracles seem to happen?

In that moment, the Father explained to me that our country has a problem with independence; in fact, we even have a Declaration of Independence. What started as a noble revolution and the founding of our nation turned into something else. Sometimes things that start out as a positive force, even a unifying one, can ultimately be a negative spirit.

Bleeding Purple

I've lived in Minnesota almost my whole life, and I am a true Minnesotan through and through. Like any good Minnesotan, I am a die-hard Minnesota Vikings football fan. It has been said that people in Minnesota bleed purple. Unfortunately, as a Viking's fan, there has been a lot of bleeding! When I was a teenager, and even into my early twenties, I followed the Vikings wholeheartedly. I'm embarrassed to admit that it was a great day whenever the Vikings won, but when the Vikings lost, it tended to ruin my day.

It got to the point where the Lord himself had to confront me on this issue. He said, "Jonnyboy, you either need to watch the Vikings for enjoyment, or you need to stop watching the Vikings." He is a good daddy, and this was a moment of tough love. You will be happy to know that I chose the former rather than the latter. My wife will testify that there was a shift that took place that day, and I can now watch the Vikings because I like football and enjoy spending time with my family. I'm happy to report that my mood is no longer affected by the outcome of a football game! I know this is a silly example, but I want to illustrate that even football, which is not inherently evil, can be a negative spirit.

Here is a more insidious example. Being religious is a noble thing. Adhering to something you believe in, and following it with discipline and passion, is a wonderful endeavor, but, when discipline and rules become more important than love and people's hearts, religion can become a religious spirit, and it is clear in the gospels that Jesus is not a fan of the religious spirit.

Declaration of Independence

The Declaration of Independence began as a positive force and righteous political action. John Hancock, the first signer of the Declaration of Independence, wrote, "Resistance to tyranny becomes the Christian and social duty of each individual...Continue steadfast and, with the proper sense of your *dependence* on God, nobly defend those rights which heaven gave, and no man ought to take from us."

John Hancock understood that a declaration of independence could be powerful and dangerous. He also understood that independence from a tyrannical king was noble but declaring independence from everyone and anything, including God, could be trouble. This is certainly true in the United States, and I would surmise this is true all across the world.

As Americans, we put such a premium on the word "independence." From childhood, we are indoctrinated with the value of independence. It has become synonymous with the "American dream." We value independent living and independent goals. We aspire to be independently wealthy and look down on inheritances and trust funds. Simply put, we don't need anyone.

God told me that day, while I was riding the lawn mower, that He is completely willing and able to plunder the forces of darkness. He is not intimidated by dark places. However, in the United States, there is a spirit of independence, and God will never force Himself on anyone. There has always been two trees to choose from. We would love to see crazy miracles, but we are not desperate or dependent on them.

I've heard it said that "the kingdom is drawn toward hunger, and when we are fed in the kingdom, we do not become satisfied, we become hungrier." If I can be so bold, we, in the United States, are satisfied. We are not hungry, and, in fact, we don't need anyone.

Declaration of Dependence

Here is an important biblical truth: There is not a single place in the Bible where independence is promoted. "God helps those who help themselves" is not in the Bible! Never in history has the Father wanted us to be independent. In fact, the opposite is true. He always wants us completely dependent on Him, always in a relationship with Him.

As stated in the last chapter, He creates a culture where we are to be interdependent on one another.

> For by one Spirit we were all baptized into one body—whether Jews or Greeks, whether slaves or free—and have all been made to drink into one Spirit. For in fact the body is not one member but many. If the foot should say, "Because I am not a hand I am not of the body," is it therefore not of the body? And if the ear should say, "Because I'm not an eye I am not of the body," is it therefore not of the body? If the whole body were an eye, where would be the hearing? If the whole were hearing where would be the smelling? But now God has set the members, each one of them in the body just as He pleased. And if they were all one member, where would the body be? But now indeed there are many members, yet one body. And the eye cannot say to the hand, "I have no need of you;" nor again the head to the feet, "I have no need of you." (1 Corinthians 12:13–21)

Co-mission vs. Self-Mission

I believe the independent spirit is one of the main subcategories of the orphan spirit. An orphan operates under self-rule, lacks trust in others, and tends to live life isolated and afraid. The most devastating effect in our world today and in society has been the infiltration of the independent spirit into marriages. How can marriages today fully embrace their co-mission and strive toward unity of purpose when they have not only succumbed to the independent spirit but have also embraced it?

As mentioned before, a loving father puts boundaries around his children. He doesn't put boundaries around his children to control them or to stifle them. Within a boundary, there is complete freedom. We try to equate independence with freedom, and we fail to realize that true freedom comes through dependence on the Father and the loving boundaries that He places around us.

Once again, the key to embracing dependence on the Father is defining our identity in Him. It is critical that all of our marriages embrace the culture of dependency. The culture of dependency is inherent in the co-mission. There are things that can only be done together. This truth has no room for an independent spirit.

If we are honest, as Americans, it almost makes us cringe to think about the notion of being dependent on someone else. You may need to have the Holy Spirit examine your heart and uncover the possibility of an orphan spirit within you that longs for you to remain independent. You have to discover that maintaining an independent spirit is countercultural to what the Father originally created for His people.

In marriage, there is no room for a self-mission. To be blunt, you need to realize that you are dependent on your spouse. You are dependent on your spouse to fulfill the destiny that the Father created for your marriage—the co-mission.

The Fight for Independence

The co-mission is the entry-level step to any marriage relationship, and yet, the enemy will deter you at the first step every time if you don't fully understand your dependence on one another. Too many marriages don't make it past this step, as husbands and wives fight bitterly to maintain their independence. At the same time, they are in sorrow over the hopelessness, purposelessness, and disunity in their marriage.

The Bible makes it perfectly clear that we are called to unity, but how can we have a unity of purpose when we don't know what our co-mission is? How can we value one another when we don't realize the role that our spouses play in the co-mission?

The church also has often ignored 1 Corinthians 12; members of the congregation fight bitterly to maintain their independent views and values, not realizing that they all are members placed in the body for one purpose.

Them

Christians all over the face of the earth need to demonstrate the interdependent culture created by the Father. I am convinced it will be Christian marriages that will demonstrate it first. As you read further on in this book, it will become clear to you, as you learn more of what marriage really means, how your marriage can be a demonstration of God's culture that changes society.

This is about unity of purpose. The Father places you on this earth for a reason, and He places you in a marriage for a reason. There is work to be done for His kingdom; there are cultures that need to be reproduced and demonstrated to the world.

The world is desperate for solutions, and the institution of marriage is perhaps the most desperate. The breakthrough will occur when Christian couples discover that they are brought together for a purpose, commissioned by the Almighty God, and have work to do that requires them to work together. They are a demonstration of unity to all humankind.

I hope you're starting to understand how significant and important your marriage is. The enemy would like nothing more than your marriage to remain impotent. He would love to keep you satisfied, not hungry, just strolling through life, offering companionship to each other with no real purpose, focus, or passion.

The Father, on the other hand, wants nothing more than for you to be completely dependent on Him, because He is always loving and always perfect, and He always has in mind what's best for you. He wants you to trust Him. He wants you to let go of your independent spirit and *fully trust* Him. He also wants you to discover your co-mission, let go of your independent spirit, and fully trust your spouse. His original plan and purpose on this earth was given to *them*. His original plan never changes.

My parents never intentionally indoctrinated me with an independent spirit. This was just American culture and I was your typical all-American boy. The 1960s and 1970s ushered in an even greater deception of rebellion and independence. Following this, marriages were devastated and divorce statistics skyrocketed. This makes perfect sense in light of what the Father originally created marriage to be; once the independent spirit wrapped its tentacles around marriages, chaos ensued.

While I rode my lawn mower that day, I repented, with tears in my eyes, for the independent spirit that inhabited my life. I recommitted to my dependence on God and reaffirmed that I would listen to His voice and obey His promptings. I repented for pursuing satisfaction and comfort rather than hunger. I allowed the Holy Spirit to reexamine my life, my relationships, and my marriage. He revealed to me how I prefer to do things alone, in my own way.

I encourage you to ask the Holy Spirit to reveal the orphan areas in your life. Ask him to expose any areas of self-mission. Continue to ask the Father to displace these orphan issues with His love.

Ask your spouse to forgive you for any independent spirit that has entered into your marriage. Tell your spouse that you are committing to the co-mission and that you value the role that he or she plays in the mission. The result of this will be unity of purpose.

So many people today would be delighted to have a unified marriage; it seems to be the ultimate goal. But I will convince you that this is just the beginning. The ultimate is still ahead; let's go deeper!

6

"Help!" (I Need Somebody)
The Beatles, 1965

Understanding that the Father commissions us, as married couples, is truly an exciting and inspiring notion. In this chapter, we will go into the greater depths of intimacy as we learn more about what the Father originally created for our marriages. However, the next several chapters will begin—for some—unchartered territory. I won't present "new truth" but ancient truth that, in my opinion, was lost over time.

I hope to convince you through scripture itself of what our loving Father originally intended for our marriages. Perhaps, even more impactful than this, I will be able to testify how the application of these truths has transformed and changed everything in my own marriage.

In this chapter, we will discover the second word that represents the greater depth of intimacy that the Father intended for our marriages. We will also discover, again, that this depth of relationship reflects heaven itself.

Helper

> And the LORD God said, "It is not good that man should be alone; I will make him a *helper* comparable to him." Out of the ground the LORD God formed every beast of the field and every bird of the air, and brought them to Adam to see what he would call them. And whatever Adam called each living creature that was its name. So Adam gave names to all cattle, to the birds of the air, and to every beast of the field. But for Adam there was not found a helper comparable to him. And the Lord God caused a deep sleep to fall on Adam, and he slept and He took one of his ribs and closed up the flesh in its place. Then the rib which the LORD God had taken from man He made into a woman, and He brought her to the man. (Genesis 2:18–22)

Adam notices all of the animals have mates, but there is no one comparable to him. The Father forms woman from man and presents her to Adam. It is a beautiful demonstration of a Father caring for His children, a demonstration of a Father establishing a co-mission between a husband and wife. As mentioned in the last two chapters, it is a wonderful revelation to understand that the Father commissioned us for greatness in our marriages. However, it is not enough to know that we are commissioned; it is essential that we know our role in the commissioning.

So God made Adam a "helper comparable." The Hebrew word for helper is e*zer, kenegdo* for comparable. The word "ezer" means "strength" or "power." The word "kenegdo" means "equal" or "matching."

In the Hebrew tradition, Jewish couples physically demonstrate ezer kenegdo by standing face-to-face. They lift their hands in the air with their palms facing one another's and they lean their bodies forward with their hands together to form an arch.

The husband and wife will have strength or power that is equal, matching, and comparable in every way. In no way does the word "helper" mean "servant" or "secondary." In no way does the word "helper" mean "assistant" or "aide." In no way does the word "helper" mean the "one who carries his luggage," "pushes him along," or "holds him up." This doesn't mean there aren't times when someone assumes these roles, but simply put, it is not what the word means!

The word "ezer" means "strength" and "power." Woman is created from man to be strong and powerful; not to be secondary or inferior in strength and power, but equal to his strength and power.

This isn't my liberating idea, it is the truth from scripture.

Another Helper

Remember, the Bible repeatedly uses marriage to reflect heaven itself. The magnitude and beauty of ezer kenegdo is best demonstrated in what the New Testament says about the Helper and how it reflects what our marriages are meant to be.

> And I will pray to the Father, and He will give you *another Helper*, that He may abide with you forever—the Spirit of truth, whom the world cannot receive, because it neither sees Him nor knows Him; but you know Him, for He dwells with you and will be in you. I will not leave you orphans; I will come to you. (John 14:16–18)

> These things I have spoken to you while being present with you. But the *Helper*, the Holy Spirit, whom the Father will send in My name, He will teach you all things, and bring to your remembrance all things that I said to you. (John 14:25, 26)

> Nevertheless I tell you the truth; it is to your advantage that I go away; for if I do not go away, the *Helper* will not come to you; but if I depart, I will send Him to you. (John 16:7)

What did Jesus mean when He mentions another Helper? I believe He is referring to, as He did so many times, the book of Genesis. He is referring to the first time the Father sent a helper. The first helper is sent to the first Adam. She is taken from Adam, formed in his image, and established as his equal, comparable strength.

When Jesus refers to another Helper, He is referring to the Holy Spirit. The word "helper," from John 14, in Greek, is the word *Paraclete*. I'm sure you might have a guess as to its meaning. It is no coincidence that the word "Paraclete" means "strength" and "power!"

John 14:25,26 explains why it is good Jesus leaves; He has to leave so the Helper may come. The Holy Spirit comes not only to be with us but also to be *in* us. It is the Holy Spirit that transforms us into the image of Christ. It is that transformation that forms Jesus's bride. We, with the Holy Spirit dwelling within us, are transformed into the image of Christ with the intention for us to be His ezer kenegdo!

Just as the first Adam sees himself in the woman that is presented to him, so the second Adam is supposed to see Himself in the bride that is presented to Him. The Helper, the Holy Spirit, will transform us into Jesus's image. Just as Eve is formed in the image of Adam, so is the church fashioned in the image of Christ, and we, the bride, are comparable to Him in every way because of the Holy Spirit within us.

> But we all, with unveiled face, beholding as in a mirror the glory of the Lord, are being transformed into the *same image* from glory to glory, just as by the Spirit of the Lord.
> (2 Corinthians 3:18)

As uncomfortable as it may be to read, we, as His bride, are intended to be Christ's ezer kenegdo, His equal and comparable strength! This is only accomplished through the strength and power of *another Helper*.

As we reflect this amazing truth back toward our marriage, one simple and important question forms: Who is more strong and powerful, Jesus or the Holy Spirit? You may say this is an easy question to answer; "Neither one is more strong and powerful, they are equally strong and powerful in every way." That answer is absolutely right, and as we further explore ezer kenegdo, you will find that it is true in your marriage as well.

Submission

I encourage you to etch the image of the married couple demonstrating ezer kenegdo into your mind. I believe this picture is the best demonstration and definition of the word submission.

If you asked someone to draw a picture of their understanding of the word submission, they most likely would have someone standing tall while the other person is on their knees in a submissive pose. Most people's understanding of the word submission is that of meekness, servitude, and living "all under" someone's authority.

I believe it is time for Christian marriages to restore, redeem, and take back the word submission!

Submission is a word that belongs to family and marriages, and it should never be divisive or misused.

Submission is a spirit demonstrated by the Father, Son, and Holy Spirit, and submission is a spirit that should be demonstrated by every Christian believer.

Let's explore what the Bible says about submission in its full context. To accomplish this, it wouldn't be appropriate to pull out a few select verses from the submission section of 1 Peter. Rather, to fully understand submission, we need to dissect 1 Peter as a whole. It is always important to read scripture being mindful that the chapter breaks and verse numbers were never originally there. Sometimes these reference points can be a disservice as it brings divisions and partitions to what was intended to be a complete thought.

1 Peter begins with a beautiful description of the glorious work of Jesus Christ's death and His resurrection. Peter explains that, because of the work of Christ, we should not go back to our old ways, but through obedience we are to live with a pure heart and sincere love. Chapter 2 begins with Peter encouraging us that we are His chosen people, a chosen generation, a royal priesthood, and a holy nation. Thus, we should live before the world honorably.

With this as his introduction, Peter begins a series of instructions regarding submission:

> Therefore *submit* yourselves to every ordinance of man for the Lord's sake, whether to the king as supreme, or to governors, or to those who are sent by him for the punishment of evildoers and for the praise of those who do good. (1 Peter 2:13)

Servants, be *submissive* to your masters with all fear, not only to the good and the gentle, but also to the harsh. (1 Peter 2:18)

Wives, *likewise*, be *submissive* to your own husbands, that even if some do not obey the word, they, without a word, may be won by the conduct of their wives, when they observe your chaste conduct accompanied by fear.
(1 Peter 3:1, 2)

Husbands, *likewise*, dwell with them with understanding, giving *honor* to the wife, as to the weaker vessel, and as being heirs *together* of the grace of life, that your prayers may not be hindered. (1 Peter 3:7)

In 1 Peter 3:18–4:19, Peter explains Christ's suffering for us and stresses how we in turn should be willing to suffer for him. He exhorts us to live like Christ, with humility and serving others. Then he continues to outline his teachings specifically on submission:

Likewise you younger people, *submit* yourselves to your elders. Yes all of you be *submissive* to one another and be clothed with humility for God resists the proud, but gives grace to the humble. (1 Peter 5:1)

Peter connects his thoughts throughout this book regarding submission with the help of the word "likewise." Because of this, you can clearly see the thread he weaves throughout his message. We should operate in the spirit of submission—citizens to government, wives to husbands, husbands to wives, Christ to his church, His people to others, and younger people to their elders...

Finally the ultimate conclusion: Yes, *all* of you must be submissive to one another!

Somewhere along the line, 1 Peter 3:1 is conspicuously plucked out of the context of the entire book of 1 Peter and is used as the solitary example of submission in the body of Christ!

In my opinion, the same thing seems to happen again in Ephesians 5. Ephesians 5 is the famous chapter in the Bible about marriage. In my Bible, there is a heading to this section entitled "Marriage—Christ and the Church." Once again, the section title was not there when Paul initially wrote his letter to the Ephesians. Interestingly enough, the "Marriage—Christ and the Church" section begins at Ephesians 5:22: "Wives, *submit* to your own husbands, as to the Lord." Conventionally, this is where the teaching begins about marriage, and the verses that come before are ignored. For example, in Ephesians 5:20, 21, Paul writes, "Giving thanks always for all things to God the Father in the name of our Lord Jesus Christ, *submitting to one another* in the fear of God."

So, there it is again, Paul exhorts wives to submit to their husbands, but clearly in the context of everyone submitting to one another!

Let me provide you with a metaphor of what I feel is happening here in the teachings on submission. Let's say, as a doctor, I am delivering a message on the benefits of exercise. I explain to the entire audience that everyone should exercise because it is good for their hearts. Then, I turn my attention specifically to women and explain to them that the number one killer of women is heart disease, which is true by the way. So it is very important that women exercise. Then in turn, because I singled women out, the entire audience focuses only on the fact that it is important for women to exercise. They mistakenly conclude that it is important that *only* women exercise!

So, is it important that women submit to their husbands? Absolutely. But, it is time that I just say it, (drum roll please), so here it is...

Husbands should also submit to their wives!

So why are women singled out? I believe the reason lies with Jesus. Jesus is the most significant women liberator of all time. Because of His teaching, compassion, and blood, women are exposed to a restored culture of freedom. They had not experienced the freedom that Jesus offers since in Garden of Eden! I believe Paul felt the need to remind women that, despite this glorious freedom, they still need to submit to their husbands.

Submit One to Another

The Bible is crystal clear that we should all submit to one to another. That is the Biblical truth. Submission is a wonderful spirit that all Christians should adhere to. It is clear in 1 Peter that submission is an issue of honor and authority.

Submission and authority are given, not taken. Submission allows those to whom you give authority to speak with authority into your life. When we submit one to another (1 Peter 5:5), we release honor and authority, and give permission for those people to speak into our lives. This is true for everyone, including government leaders, husbands, wives, children, elders, bosses, parents, grandparents, pastors, and so on.

We should draw out or invoke each other's authority. Whenever we have to use scripture to invoke submission or our authority over another, we pervert the heart of scripture. I believe submission has been perverted in such a manner for far too long. Wrong theology and a misunderstanding of submission have allowed husbands to invoke their own authority over their wives.

True Submission

While the prefix "sub" means "under," I don't believe submission means to be under a person. It means to be under the "mission." To be under a person is the word "subservient." Submission in marriage does not mean

"I'm all under." True submission in marriage means "I'm all in."

How quickly our culture would change if husbands and wives looked each other in the eye in the spirit of submission and said, "I'm all in!"

How quickly our culture would change if employees looked their bosses in the eye, if citizens looked their leaders in the eye, if leaders looked their citizens in the eye, if church members looked their pastors in the eye, or if children looked their parents in the eye in the spirit of submission and said, "I'm all in!"

When submission means "I am subject to our mission," and marriages operate in ezer kenegdo, they become the perfect demonstration of submission on the earth. Just as the Trinity, which operates in equal strength, is the perfect demonstration of submission in heaven.

Submission is not a passive word; it is highly active. It is time that this word is fully restored to its beauty and efficacy.

Submission, in the true sense of the word, is the next step in our pursuit of greater depth of intimacy in our marriages. It goes a step beyond our acceptance of the co-mission, to where we are subject to the mission in equal strength and power.

Similarly to being commissioned and operating in unity, submission and equality are not unique to marriage. We should all be submissive to one another. In fact, operating in a spirit of unity and submission should, once again, be learned and practiced even before we get married. So that, when the Father does ask us to be married, we will be ready to operate in these wonderful and powerful spirits in our marriage.

The Father had such joy in His heart when He brought Adam a h*elper*. That same culture is restored to us through the blood of Jesus. It is time for our marriages to reflect the Father's heart.

It is time for you and your spouse to ezer kenegdo. Try it out. Stand toward each other, arms extended, palms touching each other, and lean in. If you are doing it right, you will feel unified, equal. If you are leaning far enough toward each other, you will feel "all in!"

In the next chapter we will once again explore the orphan spirit. You will discover how an orphan is inherently uncomfortable with submission, authority, and honor. The enemy will attempt to trick you and paralyze you here to keep you from experiencing even the greater depths of intimacy found in marriage.

7

"Bridge over Troubled Water"
Simon & Garfunkel, 1970

In the last chapter, we discovered that "helper" is the word "ezer" in Hebrew, which means "strength," and "comparable" is the word "kenegdo," which means "equal" and "matching." As you read this chapter, continue to etch in your mind the picture of ezer kenegdo: a couple touching palms to form an arch or bridge. This is the perfect illustration of equal and comparable strength. However, when the two sides are not equal, it is easy to see how the bridge would crumble.

Bridge Collapse

When one side of the bridge overpowers the other, the whole structure will collapse. When one side of the bridge doesn't fully understand their identity or what it means to submit or refuses to be "all in," it is easy to see how what is meant to be "equal and opposite" becomes "oppositional."

There is perhaps no other relationship on the face of the earth that has the potential to be as destructive and oppositional as marriage. This marriage bridge is vital to our society and the family structure, but when we see this illustrated as two sides of a bridge needing to operate in equal strength, it is easy to see why marriages are often so filled with hurt and pain.

It is quite probable that many who are reading this book are in oppositional marriages. Before we can go into the greater depths contained later in this book, it is vital that we deal with this opposition and set things back into order.

When we are in ezer kenegdo (equal strength) with our spouse, equality is a given. However, if you are having a conversation about equality without submission, then, I believe, you are having the wrong conversation. This becomes a conversation only about power. Marriage, then, is reduced to a power struggle.

I believe that truly understanding submission and what marriage was created to be is the essential target to bring healing to an oppositional marriage.

The Bible clearly states that all should be submissive to one another. I believe the Bible says that wives are to be submissive to their husbands *and* husbands are to be submissive to their wives.

As discussed in the last chapter, submission is not a passive word. It is not based on the theology of one member of a marriage bowing at the feet of the other and pretending that this is a holy position. Rather, it is assuming the position of ezer kenegdo, looking each other in the eye, and making a mutual declaration that you are "all in." This is a good start to understanding what marriage is meant to be, and it is from this position that healing and restoration will take place.

Authority Is Given

Submission is an issue of honor and authority. Submission allows those whom you give authority, to speak (with authority) in your life. According to 1 Peter 5:5, when we submit to one another, honor and authority is released. Honor and authority should never be taken, only given.

Jesus proclaims, "All authority has been *given* to Me in heaven and on earth" (Matthew 28:18). Even Jesus didn't take His authority—it was given to Him and He doesn't force that authority on us. However, He does allow us to invoke His authority. We all understand the power of praying "in Jesus's name." We would be foolish not to invoke the authority of Jesus in our lives when it has been offered as a gracious gift to us.

Similarly, I believe the Father, as a relational God, has surrounded us with others whose authority we should wisely invoke to speak into our lives. We have a mentality in our modern age that no one can tell us what to do and no one has authority in our lives. Throughout time, there has always been a push back against authority, but in the United States in the 1960s and 1970s, there was a shift that took place that proposed "no authority." This culture has put a stranglehold on relationships. Now, we, even as believers, don't know what to do with submission and authority.

Here is the hardest question to answer: Do we see our spouses as authorities in our lives? This is how the Father created it to be, and we would be exceptionally wise to invoke their authority to speak into our lives. Conversely, we would be exceptionally foolish to deny that voice access.

No one should have more authority on this earth to speak into my life than my wife. She is my ezer kenegdo, my equal and comparable strength to the bridge that we are creating for our family. If I can't trust her to provide an equal and comparable strength, then our marriage is oppositional and our bridge is in trouble.

My wife should have authority to operate in and speak into my life. That should never be a scary, dangerous proposition; it should be the reward of my submission. When marriages operate in alignment with what they were originally created to be, there will be great breakthrough, healing, restoration, and power that your marriage, perhaps, has never yet experienced!

Trust Exercise

The trouble occurs when husbands and wives simply do not trust each other. It takes about two milliseconds in marital counseling to discover that a couple lacks trust and are in opposition. However, the mistake, I believe, made in marital counseling is placing focus on the issues manifesting opposition, rather than focusing on *why* there is opposition.

Once again, it comes down to identity and the orphan spirit. If the fruit of submission is invoking others' authority and displaying honor, then those of us who struggle with an orphan spirit typically have real problems in marriage.

Orphans see authority as a source of pain. They are distrustful toward authority and tend to have a heart that resists submission. If this is true in all relationships, how much more is it true, then, in marriage? On the other hand, sons and daughters view authority with a spirit of respect and honor and see others as ministers of good in their lives.

Again, the orphan spirit within us creates a longing for others to meet our needs. When our submission is based on others meeting our needs, manipulation occurs. When our submission is based on others earning it, it's simply impossible.

If you are waiting for your spouse to meet your needs or waiting for your spouse to be perfect, you will wait forever. We can't ask our spouse to give us something that was never theirs to give. We cannot operate in the spirit of submission only when the other person is trust-worthy.

The spirit of submission is essential to the fabric of every Christian believer—and is even more essential to the fabric of every marriage. You and your spouse are co-missioned, so you chose to be subject to the mission. The platform for your mission cannot be founded upon your spouse's performance or ability to meet your need. However, most of us enter into marriage as orphans, and our marriages are built upon this very platform

The bottom line is a married orphan doesn't trust their spouse to meet their need. Make no mistake; submission is a trust exercise. "All in" means "all in."

Without a Word

When Amy and I teach this message, especially on the orphan spirit, we often have someone approach us to explain his or her oppositional marriage. For example, the wife explains to us that her husband is not "all in." She will tell us that she has tried everything to "convince" him that he needs to be more attentive to God and to her. The wife clearly sees the orphan spirit in their spouse and feels the weight of having to try to meet their needs. However, the conversation usually centers on how the spouse is actually not meeting *their* needs.

We, with the help of the Holy Spirit, do our best to try to explain to her that trust, honor, and submission are not attributes earned by her husband before she offers them to him. Submission is a spirit within us that is to be given freely.

Not only are these to be given freely, they are actually the ingredients in the recipe for a breakthrough in their marriage.

Wives, likewise, be submissive to your own husbands, that even if some do not obey the word, they, without a word, may be won by the conduct of their wives, when they observe your chaste conduct accompanied by *fear*. Do not let your adornment be merely outward—arranging the hair, wearing gold, or putting on fine apparel—rather let it be the *hidden person* of the heart, with the incorruptible beauty of a gentle and quiet spirit, which is very precious in the sight of God. For in this manner, in former times the holy women who *trusted* in God also adorned themselves, being submissive to their own husbands. (1 Peter 3:1–4)

This passage from the Bible, describing an oppositional marriage, is loaded with strategy. I believe this is completely applicable for husbands toward their wives, as well. This is a challenging, yet effective, strategy for all marriages.

This passage explains that not a word needs to be spoken to your spouse, but a demonstration of actions that comes from the Holy Spirit toward your spouse will cause transformation. The Bible is clear that nagging does not work. Only the Holy Spirit can bring transformation to your spouse's heart. "Winning" your spouse by your conduct is the goal; this is the moment when your spouse looks you in the eye and says that they are "all in."

The passage also describes chaste conduct accompanied by fear. Chaste in this case means "without frills or ornamentation." I would interpret this to mean "without manipulation." The phrase "accompanied by fear" does not mean that we should be afraid of our spouse; in this case, fear means "honor" and "respect."

The spirit of submission is found in the "hidden person of the heart." This beauty is incorruptible and precious in the eyes of God. I believe the "hidden person" is our identity. When we know who we are as sons and daughters of the most high God, then we are completely satisfied and will not look to others to meet our needs. Then, and only then, we are able to operate in a true spirit of submission toward others.

The holy women who trust in God can then be submissive to their husbands. In verse five, the women "adorn" themselves with this spirit. This of course is the Holy Spirit. I completely understand that trusting anyone, even your spouse, can be extremely difficult. The truth is, it simply can't be done by our own strength. We need to adorn ourselves in the Holy Spirit. The Holy Spirit always does the transformational work. Trusting our spouse is essential in every marriage, but the Holy Spirit needs to fill us, and we need to trust Him, which in turn gives us the strength to trust others.

I am not pretending that this is easy. For many, trust may be one of the hardest things to do.

While I believe that all marriages are restorable, some marriages and relationships are not restorable in their current state. If you are in an—physically, emotionally, or sexually—abusive relationship, then you need to seek safety for you and your children immediately. At a safe location, surround yourself with loving people and allow the Holy Spirit to bring healing to you and your spouse. Once healing has occurred, restoration and trust can once again be pursued.

Transformed People

When we allow the love of the Father to displace our orphan spirit, we will stop requiring things from others that are not theirs to give in the first place. His love will allow a freedom within our spirit that simply empowers us to *be*. This transformational love within you will be so noticeable and powerful that you will not even have to say a word to release transformation in your home. Transformed people transform marriages.

Now that I know I am a son of the most high God, and that is my identity, I can go to Him anytime and speak to Him as a son speaks to a father. Before I understood my identity, when my marriage was oppositional, I prayed to God (actually, it sounded more like complaining) about my situation. I explained to God that I was a victim and asked Him to do something about my wife. Now, when there is conflict, (yes, it still happens at times) I pray to the Father, and He gently and lovingly explains to me what is broken inside my own heart. Invariably, when I am feeling frustrated or angry toward my wife, there is actually something orphan inside of me. I ask the Father to displace it with His love, which in turn—sometimes instantaneously—transforms the way I see my wife.

Familiar Friend

I understand that we hurt each other sometimes. I understand that there are real issues that require repentance and forgiveness. The problem is, in marriages—perhaps more than any other type of relationship—we tend to hold onto these offenses. We hold onto them, protect them, nurture them, feed them, and store them for any length of time we need, and then we release them and use them to attack our spouses. We work so hard to gather and protect these offenses that it becomes extremely difficult to let them go. When these fester in our spirit, the spirit of submission becomes almost impossible.

I liken gathering offenses to wearing a satchel around your neck. It is a potential space to catalog and gather offenses and debts, which can then be used in the future as needed. The problem occurs when the satchel becomes a familiar friend. It can become part of your identity. As the satchel becomes heavier and heavier around your neck, it turns into a paralyzing, choking presence.

Submission is supposed to be about what I bring, but it becomes about what I am owed.

In order to go deeper in your marriage, you need to allow the Holy Spirit to nurture the spirit of submission within you. You cannot do it on your own strength. You need to allow the Father's love to strengthen the hidden person of your heart—your identity. This will displace the orphan spirit, which will once again allow you to trust, honor, and forgive the debt that you feel you are owed. This, in turn, will allow you to release the offenses that you have held onto for too long. If you are willing, the Holy Spirit will not only help you empty your satchel but also remove it entirely!

If it is common in your marriage to have opposition, distrust, power struggles, and dishonor, or you have never given your spouse authority to speak into your life, then remember that these are symptoms, not the problem. The problem is identity. Don't move past identity.

It is time that we take back the word submission! It is a beautiful word, and it is time that it is restored to the fullness for which it was created. When Christian marriages demonstrate true submission, all will desire it.

Unity and equality, honor and trust, commission and submission are the essential attributes to every marriage. In fact, these essential attributes are not unique only to marriage. Ideally, I believe, these should be learned prior to marriage. However, in this next chapter, we will explore a deeper intimacy that occurs on the wedding day and how marriage becomes unlike any other relationship ever created.

8

"Say You, Say Me"
Lionel Richie, 1985

We are now in the middle of discovering four words that take us to the greater depths of our marriages. The first word is "them," which encompasses the first great commission and our co-mission in marriage. The fruit of this discovery is unity of purpose. The enemy's tactic, through the orphan spirit, is the spirit of independence.

The second word is "helper," which means we are of equal and matching strength. This discovery allows us to operate in the true meaning of submission, resulting in trust, honor, and the hopeful decision to be "all in" in our marriage and allowing our spouse to have authority to speak into our lives. However, the orphan spirit wants us to remain distrustful, holding onto our offenses and relying on our own strength and manipulation.

These attributes are essential to the first steps of any marriage but are not unique to only marriage; every believer should aspire to them.

We have now arrived at the part where we discover what truly defines a marriage.

Uniquely One

This chapter discusses how a marriage between a man and woman is unlike any other relationship on the face of the earth. To begin this discussion, we have to go back to Genesis.

> And the LORD God caused a deep sleep to fall on Adam, and he slept; and He took one of his ribs, and closed up the flesh in its place. Then the rib which the LORD God had taken from man He made into a woman, and He brought her to the man. And Adam said: "This is now bone of my bones and flesh of my flesh; she shall be called Woman, because she was taken out of Man." Therefore a man shall leave his father and mother and be joined to his wife, and they shall become *one* flesh. (Genesis 2:20–24)

"They shall become one flesh," interestingly, is mentioned throughout the Bible. It is mentioned in the Old Testament, in the Gospels, and in Ephesians. This carries great importance in the narrative of marriage from the beginning of time until now. The third word on our great adventure to the greater depths of marriage is "one."

The Hebrew word for "one" is *echad*. Echad can simply mean the number "one" or "singular," but the best and most accurate interpretation of the word is actually "unique."

Deuteronomy 6:4 reads, "Hear O Israel, the LORD our God, the LORD is *One*." The word "one" here is the word "echad." With our New Testament understanding of the Trinity, it is easy to interpret echad as the Lord is singular. However, the correct interpretation is the Lord is unique. There is no one else like Him; He is completely unique!

This is the same word that is used to describe marriage in Genesis 2. When man is joined to his wife in marriage they become completely and totally unique.

Perhaps you have heard the expression "the oldest trick in the book?" Let me tell you the oldest trick in the oldest book. God, the Father, creates man from the dust of the earth and breathes life into his nostrils. From that man, He creates two human beings, man and woman. Then He introduces marriage into the culture of Eden and turns the two back into one again—no longer two individuals but *one* unique flesh, defined by and crafted upon the covenant of marriage.

You Are Me

The concept of one flesh is prevalent throughout the entire Bible, and yet I feel, today, we still do not have a firm grasp on what it means to be one flesh. We often prefer to think of it as some type of esoteric, abstract, or poetic concept when, in fact, it could not be any more concrete. When you are married, you are no longer two—you are one.

This continued misunderstanding of what it means to be one flesh is demonstrated throughout society and is repeatedly misrepresented in books and movies. In our vain attempt to romanticize the depth and intimacy of marriage, we have completely missed the mark. We hear things like "We are two pieces of a puzzle" or "We go through life singing a duet in perfect harmony" or the famous romantic line, "You complete me!" All of these sound romantic but demonstrate a complete lack of understanding of what the word "one" means. In marriage, you don't complete me, *you are me!*

We have, over time, reduced our wedding days to a meticulously planned ceremony with a reception to follow. We have, unfortunately, overlooked the monumental phenomenon that has occurred.

When my kids grow up, I may have the opportunity to speak at their wedding ceremonies. The first thing I will say at their weddings is, "You are about to witness a miracle." The wedding day is nothing short of a miracle. The very second we say, "I do," and we are pronounced husband and wife a spiritual transformation takes place: the husband in his tuxedo and the bride in her beautiful white gown, at that very moment, no longer exist; they are transformed into one flesh, completely and totally unique. Jesus addresses this very issue in Matthew 19.

The Pharisees also came to Him, testing Him, and saying to Him, "Is it lawful for a man to divorce his wife for just any reason?" And He answered and said to them, "Have you not read that He who made them at the beginning made them male and female, and said, 'for this reason a man shall leave his father and mother and be joined to his wife, and the two shall become one flesh?'" So then, they are no longer two but one flesh. Therefore what God has joined together, let not man separate. (Matthew 19:3–6)

Jesus quotes Genesis and then reiterates the quote because even He knows that it is difficult to fully comprehend and understand. When He reinforces "so then, they are no longer two but one flesh," He is explaining that a husband and wife cannot simply walk away from each other as if they are two separate individual people. God has joined them as one flesh; they are *inseparable.*

Even though you are married, don't you have your own life? Don't you have your own goals, aspirations, or dreams? Are you not your own person with your own destiny? The answer is NO! When you are married, you are one with your spouse, one flesh.

One-ification

Matthew 19:7–8 says, "They said to Him, 'Why then did Moses command to give a certificate of divorce, and to put her away?' He said to them, 'Moses, because of the hardness of your hearts, permitted you to divorce your wives, but from the *beginning* it was not so.'"

The clear shift Jesus Christ ushers in makes this verse so exciting! He not only quotes Genesis but also makes it clear again that the culture of Eden is back in play! We, once again, are to value what the Father intended from the beginning of time, and fully embrace the restoration blood that will soon be shed!

When sin and separation are introduced into the Garden of Eden, there is a clear departure from the Father's original heart and plan for marriage. The Old Testament is riddled with the culture of immorality, adultery, polygamy, harems, and concubines. Jesus comes to set things straight and brings restoration and order to the Father's original heart for marriage.

It is upon the Father's platform and perfect heart for marriage that Paul writes the famous Ephesians chapter, chapter 5, on marriage. In Ephesians 5, it is often difficult to understand if Paul is talking about marriage or the church. The clear conclusion is that he is talking about both. However, at the time of his writing this, the church is brand-new but marriage has been around for thousands of years. However, from our perspective, we may now have a better understanding of the church and realize that the institution of marriage needs to be restored.

> Be filled with the Spirit, speaking to one another in psalms and hymns and spiritual songs, singing and making melody in your heart to the Lord, giving thanks always for all things to God the Father in the name of our Lord Jesus Christ,

submitting to one another in the fear of God. Wives, submit to your own husbands, as to the Lord. For the husband is head of the wife, as also Christ is head of the church; and He is the Savior of the body. Therefore, just as the church is subject to Christ, so let the wives be to their own husbands in everything. Husbands, love your wives, just as Christ also loved the church and gave Himself for her, that He might sanctify and cleanse her with the washing of water by the word, that He might present her to Himself a glorious church, not having spot or wrinkle or any such thing, but that she should be holy and without blemish. So husbands ought to love their own wives as their own bodies; he who loves his wife loves himself. For no one ever hated his own flesh, but nourishes it and cherishes it, just as the Lord does the church. For we are members of His body, of His flesh and of His bones. For this reason a man shall leave his father and mother and be joined to his wife, and the two shall become one flesh. This is a great mystery, but I speak concerning Christ and the church. Nevertheless let each one of you in particular so love his own wife as himself, and let the wife see that she respects her husband. (Ephesians 5:18–33)

When we read this passage as a whole, it is clearly all about oneness. Paul, just like Jesus before him, quotes Genesis when he says, "For this reason the man shall leave his father and mother and be joined to his wife, and the two shall become one flesh." On our wedding day we experience "one-ification," because we have been made one.

Since Paul refers to the two becoming one flesh as a "great mystery," and marriage is so completely unique and there isn't an English word that is available to describe it, I feel empowered to make up the word "one-ification." Ephesians 5 describes what marriage will look like once it has undergone "one-ification."

Inseparable

From this context, it is essential that we examine verse 23 of Ephesians 5 closely. In my opinion, this verse has been taken out of context, and has been theologically mishandled, which has resulted in the distortion of the true meaning of this verse, and subsequently the remainder of Ephesians 5.

Verse 23 reads, "For the husband is head of the wife, as also Christ is head of the church; and He is the savior of the body."

The Greek word used here for "head" is the word *kephale* (kef-al-ay). I have great value for words and their meanings and to fully understand kephale, we must study it from a Greek perspective *and* in the context of Paul's writings.

The word "kephale" can be interpreted in two ways, metaphorically or literally. Metaphorically, the word "head" is used to symbolize leadership or rule as in the "head of the company." Another way to use it metaphorically would be in the sense of origin as in the "headwaters of a river." Alternatively, it could be used literally as the body part atop your shoulders. To determine whether this word is being used metaphorically or literally, we cannot use the modern English interpretation; rather, we must depend on how the ancient Greeks used the word "head."

In the Greek context of the New Testament, kephale has metaphorical meanings. However, "leader" or "ruler" is *not* one of them! The only Greek metaphorical connotation is that of kinship, association, and connection. For instance, a head is nothing without a body, or in regard to origin (see 1 Cor 11 regarding head coverings).

In fact, the word "kephale" is used in the Greek, almost exclusively, in a literal context, as a head attached to a body. In this context, kephale is best described as "inseparable."

To use the word "leader" whenever reading the word "head" in an English-language New Testament is a rewriting of the scripture's text. To be clear, this isn't just a matter of two people reading the Bible's words and having a different interpretation or application, this is about knowing what the Bible's words mean.

If one reads "head" as "leader," then the remaining Ephesians passage is misinterpreted as a "leader-follower" set of instructions.

Furthermore, the best way to interpret a meaning of a word is to explore the *context* in which it is written. I encourage you to read again Ephesians 5:18–33 and see if the context fits a "ruler-follower" set of instructions or if it is describing a marriage that is "one and inseparable."

If one reads "head" as being "joined inseparably," the passage becomes more clear and coherent. The whole concept of Ephesians 5 is not one of being a leader or ruler over the other, but rather, one being inseparable from the other. Paul is describing "one-ification."

To see this any other way leaves Ephesians 5:29 awkwardly out of context: "After all, no one ever hated their own body, but they feed and care for their body, just as Christ does the church." If you read "head" as "leader," you are left with the interpretation that perhaps leaders are responsible for feeding and caring for their subordinates. But if this were true, there would be no need to mention being joined together—or love, for that matter. Since "head" means joined together, inseparably, the verse fits the context quite well.

Paul points out to those in Ephesus, and even us today, that their ideas of marriage are completely wrong. Husbands are to look at their wives the way they look at themselves, as inseparable parts of a whole. They are to love and care for their wives the way they love and care for themselves.

This is a radical notion, especially in Greek culture and Roman law, where it was commonplace for husbands to rule over their wives. Paul uses Genesis to demonstrate to all of us that the culture of Eden, where man and woman are joined together in marriage as one flesh, is back in play.

Catering to the Curse

To reduce this passage in Ephesians 5 to a commentary about husbands as leaders or rulers is inferior and inaccurate. Rather, the higher calling for marriage is to be joined inseparably as one flesh and in the same love known by Jesus and his church.

However, a husband ruling over his wife is only mentioned in one very conspicuous place in the Bible, Genesis 3:16: "Your desire shall be for your husband and he shall rule over you."

This passage is the fall of man or the "curse," as it is often called. This is actually a warning to women against the tendency to make her relationship with her husband her primary reference point rather than her relationship with God. This clearly isn't the Father's perfect plan. Her desire and identity is meant to be found in the Father who will completely satisfy her need. Then they, as husband and wife, are to operate in oneness.

Let's be clear: The husband ruling over the wife is not the "new order," it is the "*out of order!*"

The husband as ruler over his wife is the consequence of sin. Somehow over time, and armed with Ephesians 5, we protected this wrong theology and created the wrong doctrine that sets the husband as the ruler. This teaches that the consequence of sin from the fall (i.e., curse) is acceptable, normal Christian culture! This presumes that Christ's victory over sin and the curse was to no avail, and it ignores the clear kingdom culture set forth by Christ to bring restoration and relationship back to the Father and His original plan.

How can we be commissioned, of equal strength and one flesh, and yet have one rule over the other? This is simply counterintuitive to the heart of the Father.

Liberation

So, is the whole point of "one-ification," or this book for that matter, to promote and propagate the women's liberation message? Perhaps the answer is yes, but not as we understand it. The point of the women's liberation movement is to liberate women into their own thing, apart and separate from their husbands and from men in general. I am promoting women's liberation into oneness, not independence. I believe women today are desperate to be one with their husbands, fed, nourished, and inseparable.

I believe "one-ification" establishes balance and order for both husbands and wives. I believe this culture liberates men as well. Men are liberated from an undue burden that they are solely in charge and carry the responsibility for the whole family as the "head" of said family. I believe man was never intended to do this on his own; the responsibility for the family is to be carried inseparably by the husband *and* the wife. In fact, there isn't any place in the Bible that says the man is the sole "head of the household."

Yeah—But...

I know this may be a bit unnerving, especially because we were taught that the man is the head of the household when we were still in diapers. I am sure this creates all sorts of "yeah—but..." questions. So let me address some of the most common "yeah—buts."

1. Yeah—but don't we need order in the family?

Adam and Eve are not concerned with marital order. They require nothing from each other to form their identities; they are completely satisfied in the Father's presence, and they follow His directions. The word for being "subject to the order" is "subordinate." As explained, I don't feel women were created to be man's subordinate.

   1. Yeah—but aren't you worried this will create dominating women and weak men?

This teaching does not promote women as the "head of the home" nor independent from or above her husband. It is just as countercultural and against oneness for the woman to be domineering and controlling.

   2. Yeah—but, at the end of the day, doesn't someone have to make a final decision?

Yes, that someone is you, as one flesh! A married couple should feel empowered to make mutual decisions. If you make a mutual decision, you move forward—if not, you wait. Or, because you are not orphans, you defer to the wisdom of your spouse on the matter and endorse their decision. It is a beautiful thing!

Oneness Not Sameness

Husbands and wives, in a marriage, possess different personalities, skills, graces and gifts. There will also clearly be gender differences and different roles in the way that we live our life together. Oneness does not mean sameness. But the key is to understand that these differences, skills, and abilities are no longer our own. They belong to us, as one flesh.

There are so many marriages where the husband is riddled with guilt, insecurity, and condemnation because of his failure as a leader or his wrong decisions. He has been taught since childhood that the man is the head of the household and the ruler of his wife. This errant teaching is like a millstone around his neck, as he feels the lone weight of responsibility and disappointment from the church, the leaders, and his wife, especially. While grace is needed for mistakes, there is another possible truth; this man may not have the gift of leadership! He could very well be a terrible leader, but it doesn't mean he is a terrible husband or that he doesn't care about his family.

Very often, in a similar scenario, a wife, who is gifted in administration and finance, does not feel comfortable speaking up and usurping her husband's authority. This is because, since childhood, she has been taught that the husband is the head of the home and the ruler of his wife. This errant teaching also feels like a millstone around her neck since she often feels helpless, disappointed, and bitter. This doesn't make her a terrible, rebellious wife. She's not operating in the "Jezebel spirit;" her family is simply not utilizing or appreciating her gift.

This is what wrong theology encourages. It chokes and paralyzes. The enemy loves it when we get distracted and operate outside of the Father's original heart and plan.

How different this marriage would look if this husband and wife understood who they are as one flesh. If this wife appreciated her husband for the gifts and talents he *does* have rather than depreciate him due to the gifts he lacks, the whole family would reap the benefits of his talents and unique contributions. If this wife—without guilt—with the support of her husband, administrates the family, then she would be empowered in her gift, and the family would operate in order and peace. This in no way implies that the wife, or the husband, in this relationship should operate outside of their spouse's blessing or in rebellion. They are one flesh, nothing can be done apart from one another; they are inseparable.

This is why marriage is a covenant. Covenant means "all that I have is yours and all that you have is mine." In a very real sense, marriage is a double portion—all that I have *in addition* to all that you have. Oneness allows the fullness of the double portion.

Becoming one flesh with your spouse may sound intimidating, but I assure you, it is rewarding and glorious.

How can we go deeper into marriage when we don't understand what marriage really is? Our wedding day is a really big deal. If your wedding was anything like mine, you probably didn't understand what you were signing up for. The person you were before no longer exists. You are one flesh, completely unique.

Also, if your wedding was anything like mine, you were probably married as orphans, immediately requiring things from your spouse that was never theirs to give. Needless to say, the orphan spirit will have real problems with the concept of one flesh, as we will discuss in the next chapter. To truly pursue oneness, we will have to confront, and have the Holy Spirit displace, this orphan spirit at an even deeper level.

9

"Leader of the Pack"
The Shangri-Las, 1964

In medical school, I learned that if the instructor repeated something, it was probably on the test and deserved my attention. I always love it when there are repeated themes drawn throughout the entire Bible. Because those themes tend to carry such significance, they deserve our special attention. I believe that one of the significant themes, which is initially mentioned in Genesis, restored by Jesus in the Gospels, and reemphasized by Paul later in the New Testament, is "a man shall leave his father and mother and be joined to his wife, and they shall become one flesh."

I can't begin to imagine the importance and potency our marriages will have when we fully embrace the reality of one flesh. We read it, hear it, and if we are honest, we often dismiss it as poetry or abstract. For families, and society for that matter, to be fully restored, I believe we need to fully embrace that we are no longer the same person as we were before we were married. Together, with our spouse, we become a unique creation, completely one, and inseparable.

This truth has nothing to do with whether you believe it, accept it, sign off on it, or even want it. This is just your reality the day you say, "I do." The decision you will need to make is whether or not you are willing to explore the fullness of what this means. The enemy would like nothing more than to keep the truth of "one flesh" hidden, diluted, and disregarded. If he can keep you as two individual, independent orphans, then he will successfully undermine the very heart of what your marriage is meant to be. If he can keep the marriage as a hierarchical "ruler versus subordinate" culture, then he will successfully perpetuate the dysfunctional cycle in marriages where we are pitted against each other.

The enemy wants to have you look at your spouse and think thoughts like "You are against me," "You are a threat to me," or "You don't understand me," and so forth. He loses the moment your eyes open and you look at your spouse with full understanding and realize, "you are me."

The purpose of this chapter is to expose the orphan spirit that battles against our "one flesh." So far, we learned that we need to first pursue position, then purpose, and then power. Our position is found in our identity as sons and daughters of the most high God. As with any orphan, who doesn't understand their position in the Father, they immediately began to compete for position.

Jockey for Position

There is no greater threat to our identity on the face of the earth than the threat from the one with whom we share our lives. There is no one who knows us better and more intimately than our spouse. So when we struggle with identity and position, it is easy to understand how we could see our spouse as a principle threat.

When we marry as orphans, we immediately begin to compete for position. Instead of establishing our position as one flesh, we jockey for position in our relationship. We immediately see our relationship as a two-lane road. Because of our individualistic and independent mind-sets, we envision marriage as two cars with two drivers on a two-lane road...and so begins the competition.

It is hard for me to admit this, but I was intimidated by my wife's greatness. It never takes long for people to get to know Amy. She is somewhat of an open book. It also doesn't take long for people to realize what an amazing, wise, and dynamic person she is. As an orphan, this was, at times, intolerable for me. I needed others to appreciate my greatness too, and the thought of her surpassing me, in any way, was inconceivable. My insecurity was not overt, but I, like most men, had tools to use to keep her in check when needed. I will discuss two tools (I'm sure there are many more) that have been used quite effectively in marriages to accomplish this very task.

One-Lane Road

The first tool—the manipulation of scripture—used primarily by men, creates a distinct advantage in this race, mainly by the perpetuation of bad theology. Our manipulation of scripture results in a culture where there are two separate cars on the road, and the wife is not allowed to pull into the lead. To take the analogy one step further, I would add that the wife isn't allowed to drive at all. Her role is to be the misinterpreted version of the helper. Her position is to be, at the best, in the passenger seat, more typically in the backseat, and if she is truly submissive, outside of the car, in the back, pushing.

I believe this has been perpetuated by a patriarchal Old Testament mind-set that women are subordinate property. I think all would agree that this was not the original loving heart of the Father or the culture He created in the garden. However, when one group of people, especially those in charge, is happy and content with the way things are, they stop asking questions.

Take slavery for example. Slavery was acceptable for a long period of time because those with power were profitable and content with the practice. They stopped asking questions about whether it was moral or Biblical. They argued that slavery is in the Bible so it must be acceptable. However, once someone like William Wilberforce was brave enough to question the practice, the morality, and Biblical fortitude of the matter it was then explored. The Bible mentions slavery but in no way endorses it, and the morality of enslaving another is clearly rejected.

I believe there has been a bondage placed on women, and it is time we begin to ask questions to break those bonds. We need to not just believe what we have always heard but study scripture, where we will find that husbands and wives are equal, unified, and one flesh.

If you concede this point, then you may feel that we should restore the culture of marriage, where husbands and wives drive down a two-lane road side by side, completely equal, unified in direction—not one pulling ahead of the other. If this is the way you see it, then you are still missing the whole point!

Marriage is not a two-lane road with two cars and two drivers! Marriage is a one-lane road with one car and one driver—you as husband and wife, one flesh. There is no backseat and no passenger seat; there is just one seat!

If our conversation is only about equality and unity, two cars driving side by side, then we are having the wrong conversation. This goes much deeper than equality or unity—this is about oneness, the miracle that occurs on the wedding day. Two become one. There is no other human relationship like this; this is marriage, completely unique and completely one.

The Shovel

The second tool is criticism. Criticism accomplishes two things. First, it puts you ahead and your spouse behind. Second, as an orphan, it is imperative to let our spouse know that everything is not OK. We don't want our spouse to feel too comfortable or complacent in their role of meeting our needs. This is why we tend to hurt the one we love the most with our words.

Ephesians 5:26 explains that we are sanctified (which means to "set apart") by our word. To set someone apart by our word implies promotion and encouragement. Our words are nourishment. Our words should be a shovel, used to create a hill for our spouse upon which they stand higher. Alternatively, our words can be used as a shovel to dig a hole that brings our spouse lower. Criticism contains words we use to tear another down and keep ourselves in the lead on the road.

The Bible says, "But no man can tame the tongue. It is an unruly evil, full of deadly poison" (James 3:8). Ephesians 5 says that we are to "nourish" her, not poison her. We are to "sanctify and cleanse her with the washing of water by the word." Our words are to bring life and sanctity, not death and destruction.

Our spouse is not the enemy. Our spouse is not a threat. Our spouse is not against us. Our spouse *is* us. Until we fully understand this, we will continue to jockey for position.

This implies that when my wife hurts, I hurt. When she is joyful, I am joyful. When I speak rudely to her or criticize her, my brokenness and lack of oneness is revealed.

My wife no longer threatens me. Because I am completely satisfied in the presence of my Papa, and I require nothing from her for my worth or identity, I can now celebrate her greatness. Rather than rule over her, I enthusiastically promote her and cheer her on as she runs with Him! As we pursue oneness, we don't have to compete with one another, we *are* one another!

Name Change

Remember, first, position, then purpose, and then power. Our position in marriage is found in oneness. The fruit of this is unity of purpose and equal in power. Do women want equality? If so, it is not found in independence or power, but in becoming one flesh. Purpose and power should always flow from our position. There is no better example of this than what is demonstrated in the very first marriage as told in Genesis.

> Out of the ground the LORD God formed every beast of the field and every bird of the air, and brought them to Adam to see what he would call them. And whatever Adam called each living creature that was its name. So Adam gave names to all cattle to the birds of the air, and to every beast of the field. But for Adam there was not found a helper comparable to him. And the LORD God caused a deep sleep to fall on Adam, and he slept; and He took one of his ribs and

closed up the flesh in its place. Then the rib which the LORD God had taken from man He made into a woman, and He brought her to the man. And Adam said: "This is now bone of my bones and flesh of my flesh; she shall be called *Woman*, because she was taken out of Man." Therefore a man shall leave his father and mother and be joined to his wife, and they shall become one flesh. (Genesis 2:19–24)

Adam is given the charge to name each living creature. After the divine surgeon completes His work and creates woman from man, I can imagine His pride, as a father, when He presents her to Adam.

It is such a beautiful moment. When Adam sees himself in the woman—the beauty of the Father's creation—he names her based upon her position as his "one flesh." Notice that in verse 22 the word "woman" is not capitalized: "Then the rib of which the LORD God had taken from man He made into a woman." However, in verse 23 when Adam proclaims, "She shall be called Woman," the word "woman" is capitalized because it is now her proper name. Interestingly, it isn't Adam and Eve who inhabit the garden at all; it is Adam and Woman. They are completely satisfied in the Father's presence. They know their identity in the Father, and they know their identity as one flesh in marriage.

It isn't until the original sin and the fall of humankind occurs that Woman's name is tragically changed.

And Adam called his wife's name Eve, because she was the mother of all living. Also for Adam and his wife the LORD God made tunics of skin, and clothed them. Then the LORD God said, "Behold the man has become like one of Us to know good and evil. And now, lest he put out his hand and take also of the tree of life, and eat, and live forever"—therefore the LORD God sent him out of the Garden of Eden to till the ground from which he was taken. So He drove out the man; and He placed cherubim at the east of the Garden of Eden, and a flaming sword which turned every way, to guard the way to the tree of life. (Genesis 3:20–24)

The heartbreaking consequences of sin are already evident, and the immediate effect on marriage is devastating. Adam initially names his wife Woman based on her position and her identity as one flesh. After the fall, her name is changed to Eve, which means "the mother of all living." This name sadly demonstrates a loss of identity and intimacy, because now she is named based on her purpose.

They are also compassionately removed from their precious home, so they cannot eat of the tree of life, and are forever separated from the loving Father.

This tragic transformation is evident all throughout the Old Testament; both in the way men treat women and in the sorrow and shame felt by women when they are barren. When their existence and identity is based on purpose rather than position, it is easy to see why barrenness equates to worthlessness.

However, as New Testament believers, we are not trapped in a culture of worthlessness! Jesus is the most powerful and compassionate liberator to have ever walked the face of the earth. He came to not only destroy the wages of sin and death but also to restore the Father's original heart and plan for His people, for families, and for every marriage.

It is so imperative that men, women, husbands, and wives understand and fully embrace their identity as sons and daughters of the loving and compassionate Father. This, in turn, will allow us to bear our true and real name based on our identity and our position. It is only through this revelation and the work of the Holy Spirit that every marriage can be restored to its fullness.

We need to continue to allow the Father's love to displace the orphan spirit within us so we don't try to have our spouse meet the needs that can only be met by the Father.

Our battle is never with flesh and blood, which includes your spouse. It is the enemy that loves to keep us orphan and loves to keep division alive in our marriages through our actions and our words. We need to break the cycle of criticism and realize that it is not "you versus me" but "you are me."

The spirit of "one-ification" is unique. It can only happen in marriage. If you are married, then it happened on your wedding day! Maybe you didn't know what you were getting yourself into, but I am confident, if I did my job, that you will no longer read the words "one flesh" in a fast, drive-by manner. Rather, my prayer is that you will pause at the seriousness, importance, and gloriousness of the phrase, and you will appreciate and pursue the uniqueness that you possess as husband and wife!

Initially, we learned the framework, or the initial steps, of establishing a marriage, discovering the privilege of being commissioned and the honor demonstrated through the spirit of submission. We discussed the absolute miracle that occurs on the wedding day when we no longer are two and become completely unique as one flesh.

One-ification is amazing, but in the last two chapters we get to move beyond the implications of the wedding day to the culture of marriage itself. Our loving Father created a greater depth of intimacy that is found only in marriage. Deep intimacy is where marriage actually becomes the ultimate marriage!

10

"How Deep Is Your Love"
Bee Gees, 1977

We are now at the most exciting part of this book and the most intimate part of marriage. We have laid the framework, explored what actually happens when we get married, and celebrated the incredible miracle that occurs when we say, "I do." Now comes the adventure—a marriage that is lived together as one flesh.

Before we dive deeper, let's have one last review. The start of the relationship happens when we realize that we have been *commissioned*. The first co-mission is not given to only one person; it is given to *them*. We should be excited at the notion that there are things to be done for the kingdom that can only be done together. Marriage is built upon this premise and demonstrates heaven by creating a unity of *purpose*.

We are to approach the relationship with the spirit of *submission*. By understanding the word "helper," we know that we are equipped with equal and comparable strength, and we can freely submit ourselves to one another. This creates a culture in marriage where we are "all in" or subject to the mission. Marriage is also built upon this premise and demonstrates heaven by the *power* of honor and authority.

Then there is the actual wedding day, which is the moment when something truly miraculous takes place. We are no longer two independent individuals. After our wedding day, we are *one* flesh. This demonstration of "one-ification" reflects our God in His Triune relationship and is completely unique and found in no other relationship on earth.

If you have embraced the pathway that got us here, then you may be content with a marriage that demonstrates equality, unity, and oneness. However, there is still the ultimate depth of intimacy for us to uncover, and to explore this greater depth of the Father's love, let's once again go back to His original heart found in Genesis.

> Then the LORD God took the man and put him in the Garden of Eden to attend and keep it. And the LORD God commanded the man, saying, "Of every tree of the garden you may freely eat; but of the tree of the *knowledge* of good and evil you shall not eat, for in the day that you eat of it you shall surely die." (Genesis 2:15–7)

And Adam said, "This is now bone of my bones and flesh of my flesh; she shall be called Woman, because she was taken out of Man." Therefore a man shall leave his father and mother and be joined to his wife, and they shall become one flesh. *And they were both naked, the man and his wife, and were not ashamed.*
Now the serpent was more cunning than any beast of the field which the LORD God had made. And he said to the woman, "Has God indeed said, 'You shall not eat of every tree of the garden?'" And the woman said to the serpent, "We may eat the fruit of the trees of the garden; but of the fruit of the tree which is in the midst of the garden, God has said, 'You shall not eat it, nor shall you touch it, lest you die.'"

Then the serpent said to the woman, "You will not surely die. For God knows that in the day you eat of it your eyes will be opened, and you will be like God, *knowing* good and evil." So when the woman saw that the tree was good for food, that it was pleasant to the eyes, and a tree desirable to make one wise, she took of its fruit and ate. She also gave to her husband, and he ate. Then the eyes of both of them were opened, and they *knew* that they were naked; and they sewed fig leaves together and made themselves coverings. And they heard the sound of the LORD God walking in the garden in the cool of the day, and Adam and his wife hid themselves from the presence of the LORD God among the trees of the garden. The LORD God called to Adam and said to him, "Where are you?" So he said, "I heard your voice in the garden, and I was afraid because I was naked; and I hid myself." And He said, "Who told you that you were naked? Have you eaten from the tree of which I commanded you that you should not eat?" Then the man said, "The woman whom you gave to be with me, she gave me of the tree, and I ate." And the Lord God said to the woman, "What is this you have done?" The woman said, "The serpent deceived me and I ate." (Genesis 2:23–3:13)

And Adam called his wife's name Eve, because she was the mother of all living. Also for Adam and his wife the Lord God made tunics of skin, and clothed them. (Genesis 3:20, 21)

The Naked Truth

If I were to summarize these passages, I would say that they were about *nakedness*. Genesis 2:25 is the key passage: "And they were both naked, the man and his wife, and were not ashamed." This Bible passage is the cultural summary of the Garden of Eden. The Father creates a culture on this earth where men and women will not only to be completely naked but completely without shame.

Now let's be clear, while I am advocating the restoration of the culture of Eden, I am not proposing a revolution of nudist colonies! However, the implication of Adam and Eve being naked goes way beyond physical clothing and speaks directly to the deeper culture of Eden. The greater implication of this passage is that they were without coverings and knew no shame. This is the true culture of Eden, one that I absolutely want to see restored! This becomes much clearer when we see what happens after they disobey the Lord.

> Then the eyes of both of them were opened, and they knew that they were naked; and they sewed fig leaves together and made themselves coverings. And they heard the sound of the LORD God walking in the garden in the cool of the day, and Adam and his wife hid themselves from the presence of the LORD God among the trees of the garden. Then the LORD God called to Adam and said to him, "Where are you?" So he said, "I heard Your voice in the garden and I was afraid because I was naked; and I hid myself." (Genesis 3:7–10)

I find this portion of the passage fascinating. When they know they are naked, they fashion coverings out of fig leaves and hide from *each other* first. Then they hide themselves from God's presence because they are naked; but wait a minute, they aren't naked—they are covered by fig leaves! You see, it is *shame*—not physical nakedness—that motivates them to hide from the Father's presence. Something dramatic has changed. Being "naked and unashamed" is the created culture of intimacy, and in a moment that intimacy is lost.

We are composed of spirit, soul, and body. The nakedness Adam and Woman experience is first a spiritual nakedness. God is a spirit, and that is why they hide their nakedness from Him, even though they are not physically naked.

Who Knew?

The created culture of deep intimacy is called "consummation." It is in this deep intimacy that marriage becomes a marriage. Consummation means "crescendo," "grand finale," or, the best interpretation, "the ultimate." Consummation is *the ultimate* goal of intimacy for every marriage.

To examine the nature of this ultimate intimacy, which was created and then lost, we need to explore one last keyword. The keyword is "knew." You probably are more familiar with this word in the context of Genesis 4:1: "Now Adam *knew* Eve his wife, and she conceived and bore Cain, and said, 'I have acquired a man from the LORD.'"

The word "knew" in Hebrew is the word *yada*. The word "yada" can be used to describe the sexual act in marriage as referenced in Genesis 4. However, yada is much greater in scope than just the physical act of sex. In fact, when we look at previous passages in Genesis 2 and 3, "yada" is the same word used for "knowledge," "knowing," and "knew" in the "tree of the *knowledge* of good and evil," "you will be like God, *knowing* good and evil," and "they *knew* that they were naked."

"Yada" is a gigantic word; it is not limited to a sexual relationship or your intellect. The consummation of a marriage goes way beyond a physical experience. Yada is best described as a "deeply intimate experience."

Another great example of the word "yada" is found in Matthew 7:22, when Jesus says, "Many will say to me in that day, 'Lord, Lord, have we not prophesied in Your name, cast out demons in Your name, and done many wonders in Your name?' And then I will declare to them, 'I never *knew* you; depart from Me, you who practice lawlessness!'"

This is the same word used in Genesis. He isn't implying that he didn't understand who they were, or that He lacked intelligent recognition. Jesus explains that our actions, our works, and our understanding are not sufficient for a kingdom relationship. He requires a deep intimate experience with us; he asks us to "yada" with Him.

Good and Evil

With this understanding of the word "yada" in mind, let's explore exactly what happens in Genesis 3, something that starts so gloriously and ends in shame and hiding.

The story begins with the tree of the knowledge of good and evil. A conventional understanding of this tree might be that there is something in the substance of the fruit, that, when eaten, makes Adam and

Woman smarter or more knowledgeable about the issues of good and evil. Perhaps it may expose them to a greater understanding of the cosmos, and perhaps the Lord forbids the eating of this fruit because He wants to spare them the pain of learning about evil. Others have interpreted this as simply knowing right from wrong. However, I feel that this is not what the tree is about.

    Let's review what we know so far. Knowledge is the word "yada," which implies a deep intimate experience. Where has there been any references to the word "good" thus far in Genesis? The word "good" is used many times as an adjective to describe God's creation. Evil has just come on the scene and is found in Satan himself in the form of a serpent. So, it is the tree of the knowledge (yada) of good (creation, humankind) and evil (Satan).

    I don't know if there is anything magical about the tree or if it is just a boundary of obedience placed in the garden by the loving Father who gave us free will, but He warned Adam that having a deep intimate experience (yada) with evil would change everything. This shift takes place when good "yadas" with evil. They heed the voice of evil, obey that voice, and consummate with evil!

    This is a key point. Adam and Woman know they are naked because their accuser tells them they are. Satan's tactics never change: he tempts you and then accuses you. How do I know this? Because it is written in Genesis 3:10, 11: "'I was afraid because I was naked; and I hid myself.' And He said, 'Who told you that you were naked?'"

Their intimacy with evil allows his influence and voice into theirs lives. The Bible says their eyes are opened (they no longer see an innocent, friendly serpent) and their ears are opened (he tells them they are naked). I would guess that Satan doesn't stop there. He most likely tells them they are failures and mistakes, and that God will be so mad they better go hide.

Nakedness was cultural. It only becomes countercultural when they yada with evil. Man introduces sin and death into what has been good, and the future of Eden tragically changes.

Sin is the offspring of a consummated relationship between good and evil.

You Are What You Eat

Consummation is the deep, ultimate intimacy in a marriage. I was fascinated when I realized the root word of consummation is "consume." Do you see the connection? They can look at the tree, admire it, even touch it, but they cannot consume it. If they consummate with evil through disobedience and rebellion, they will surely die because the "wages of sin is death." (Romans 6:23) Furthermore, this decision keeps humankind hiding in shame from God, separates them from His heart, and transfers dominion of the earth from good (humankind) to evil (Satan). Every subsequent child born is born into a sinful nature (or culture), and into a world of darkness.

I believe this is the main connotation of Genesis 3:15: "And I will put enmity between your seed (humankind born into sin) and her Seed (the One who would save us from that sin)" and Genesis 3:16: "I will greatly multiply your sorrow and your conception; in pain you shall bring forth children."

I don't think this speaks of painful deliveries, but rather the sorrow in a mother's heart to deliver a child into a world of sin and darkness. Eve experiences this pain in the first generation when Cain kills Abel!

When man yadas with evil, what is lost is the culture of nakedness, the culture of intimacy. What is lost is a unique culture afforded to marriage, marked and defined by being unashamed.

Even if they didn't sin, we can't be certain if Adam and Woman would have covered their naked bodies once they began to have children and start a family culture. We only know the Father created them naked in a unique marriage culture. Regardless, I'm convinced that they would have continued to be naked in their spirits and souls, and they would never have covered their bodies out of shame but out of intimacy and the desire for privacy and exclusivity. I am convinced that their physical nakedness would continue as an essential component of the culture of their marriage intimacy.

Physical nakedness today should be enjoyed in every marriage without any shame. However, it is important to note that, because physical nakedness was created in context of a marriage culture, we should never look at or exploit nakedness in anyone who is not our spouse. This includes nudity in movies, magazines, in premarital intimacy, and the like. Also, the bedroom is a married couple's Garden of Eden, and their intimacy should be private and never loosely discussed with others.

Intimacy Lost

There are three signs that the first marriage would quickly unravel and the culture would rapidly turn to wickedness. The first sign comes when they hide from each other before they hide from God! Second, as mentioned before, Adam changes Woman's name to Eve, which is a heartbreaking loss of intimacy. Third, God warns Woman in Genesis 3:16: "Your desire shall be for your husband, and he shall rule over you." Desire means "from the Father." She should have found worth and identity in the presence of the Father, but now she will try to find it in her husband. Now that she is orphaned, she will look to her husband to meet her needs. The consequence of this misguided approach is that he will rule over her!

One ruling over the other isn't a position of intimacy. It doesn't take long in the continuing story of Genesis before we begin to see the subservient role of women manifested.

Restoration of Intimacy

Today, we live on the other side of the cross! We need to see that the goal isn't just healthy marriages but restored marriages. This is about culture! This is about the Father's original culture that is straight from His heart.

The second Adam accomplishes what the first could not. Jesus is subjected to the same temptation and perversion of evil, but He never consummates it. In 2 Corinthians 5:21 it says, "For He made Him who *knew* no sin to be sin for us, that we might become the righteousness of God in Him." Jesus never yadas with evil, and He never allows the seed or voice of evil a place of intimacy in His life.

Jesus frees us from the bondage of sin and desires for us to enter into an intimate relationship with Him. I believe this explains the difficult passage in John 6:56: "He who eats My flesh and drinks My blood abides in Me, and I in him." To find that place of deep intimacy where He abides in me and I in Him, I need to consume Him! It is an invitation to consummation and restoration, the ultimate in intimacy. Jesus is the tree of life; we consume Him and live forever!

The blood that Jesus shed isn't just to save us, but to restore His Father's culture! His blood is more than enough to accomplish this. He wants to restore the culture of Eden for every marriage, which is defined by a pure, deep intimacy and a culture where they are naked and unashamed.

Without a doubt, Jesus not only came on a salvation mission but also a restoration mission. Luke 19:10 *doesn't* say that Jesus came to seek and save the lost; it says, "For the Son of Man has come to seek and save *that which was lost."*

This entire chapter is dedicated, in great detail, to that which is lost! Do you believe there is still more to be restored in your marriage? Genesis 3 still has an effect on marriages today, despite the fact that the Seed has already come to usher in restoration.

We get a glimpse of its glory in Genesis 1 and 2, and then we need to pursue the cultural restoration for our own marriage afforded to us by the blood of Jesus.

So what are we pursuing? We are pursuing the culture of Eden where Adam and Woman are *naked and unashamed*. To achieve this culture, we will have to do a very difficult thing: *take off our coverings*. The goal is intimacy.

We have to start with shame. When we are filled with shame, we fashion ourselves coverings and hide. However, when we are covered and hidden, we cannot be intimate. In other words, when we are unashamed, we can be naked, when we are naked, we can be intimate.

This will require a lot of work, but rest assured, not by you. The Holy Spirit gets to do the work, you just have to be willing and want this for your marriage.

As discussed in this chapter, the orphan spirit so overtly injected its influence in the first marriage, causing the culture of intimacy to be lost in the garden. In the last chapter, we will once again explore the effect of the orphan spirit on our marriages today in regard to intimacy. We will see how the issues we equate with intimacy, such as love and sex, are influenced by the contrasting cultures. I will offer some practical suggestions to help overcome shame, allowing you to truly be consummated—the ultimate in intimacy!

11

"If You Don't Know Me by Now"
Simply Red Toy Soldiers, 1989

It is very unusual to read a book about marriage and not even address love or sex until the last chapter! Perhaps, this is purposeful, because, as a reminder, we are pursuing the culture of marriage. I would say that love and sex don't create the culture of a marriage—they are the outpouring of that culture.

You see, our Father, is the creator of all things. Not surprisingly, that includes love and sex. As discussed previously, we are to connect with Him as our source of love and identity. God is a spirit and our connection to Him is through our spirit. We are created with a spirit, soul, and body. It often works in that order. What fills our spirit will ultimately fill and affect our soul (mind, will, emotions, feelings) and this, in turn, will manifest through our bodies (in our words and actions).

This is why scripture says, "Out of the abundance of the heart the mouth speaks" (Matthew 12:34). This truth confirms the notion that whatever is filling our spirit and soul will ultimately come out of our body.

What's Love Got to Do with It?

Since I had fun researching *Billboard*'s No. 1 hits as my chapter titles, let me include one more, "What's Love Got to Do with It?" sung by Tina Turner circa 1985. In the song, Tina concludes that love is just a "second-hand emotion."

Sorry Tina, love is not an emotion or a feeling. Love is actually a person. You have heard it said that God is love. This simple truth is actually simply true. All of the love ever experienced on this earth is contained in, and expressed through, the Almighty God. Jesus is the embodiment of that love. Love is why He was sent to us (John 3:16), and it is what He demonstrates here on earth through His death and resurrection. Through Him all things were created, including us, and including love. Because He is the source of all love, He has given us access to His unending reservoir!

Once again, we access that reservoir through an intimate, personal relationship with the Father Himself. We will find ourselves completely satisfied in the love of our Father. Then, when our spirit is filled with His love, our souls will be fed. Our mind, will, emotions, and feelings are then the byproduct of that satisfaction and the love we feel in our spirit. That same created love is then expressed through our bodies, words, and actions.

It is only through our intimate relationship with the true love-giver that we can enter into the ultimate intimate relationship (yada) with our spouse. So, my apologies to Tina Turner, once we know what love is and where it came from, it has everything to "do with" our marriage!"

When we fully understand that we are sons and daughters of the truly loving Father, then the expression of our love is *the fruit and not the fuel*. Orphans, on the other hand, are disconnected from the source of love. Sin and shame cause them to hide from the loving Father rather than receive His love. Orphans are innately uncomfortable with love. They try to tap into their own strength, will, and emotions to somehow "create" love. They hope their love will somehow fuel the relationship. That is why the vast majority of the people in this world, including Christians, think love is an emotion.

When an orphan enters into marriage, he or she *requires*. They desperately try to have their spouse meet their needs. Their spouse may be able to meet their needs for a time, but then disenchantment enters and marriages quickly fall into a tailspin. Orphans have needs that spouses can never meet and broken things that spouses can never fix.

There is a new trend in weddings today that may turn your stomach a bit. Instead of declaring the vow, "Until death do us part," couples vow, "Until love runs out." There is an obvious sorrow and sadness to this illustration, but it makes perfect sense. People today, as orphans, can only offer their spouse the love that comes from their soul. It is a resource limited by their strength and will. When this fuel dries up, as it inevitably will, the marriage will have lost its strength and meaning, and the individuals will need to look elsewhere to have their needs met. Or, equally as common, the marriage downshifts to that of low expectation, negligible passion, survival mode, and loss of intimacy, and many couples simply ride the marriage out with the "low-fuel light" on.

So, the answer to this problem is not vain attempts to strengthen our soul! We often try to tackle our issues and problems by attacking the issues and problems. We think that the trajectory of our marriages will change by fixing the conflicts in marriage or by providing "fix-it" tools. In my experience, so often the problem isn't the problem. It is just the symptom. We need to stop trying to fix the symptoms and start trying to cure the disease. Hopefully by now, you can predict what the disease is. The disease is the orphan spirit and it can only be cured, or displaced, by an unbridled baptism of love with the Father and the discovery of your identity as a son or daughter. The root of the disease is in your spirit!

I tend to get frustrated with conventional Christian counseling that focuses on the problems and symptoms of dysfunction in a marriage. All that "improved communication" accomplishes is an opportunity and a platform for one spouse to air their disappointments, complaints, and criticisms to the other spouse, and then try to implement strategies or tools to try to meet that spouse's orphan needs.

You may be familiar with the "five love languages." I believe this could potentially be a helpful tool in marriage, but from my perspective, I believe this is more often used as "orphan languages." No matter how perfectly or frequently a spouse uses words of affirmation, quality time, gift giving, acts of service, or physical touch, it will never be enough to satisfy their spouse's needs. Once again, it is an attempt to try to "love better" through our souls and bodies. Many well-intentioned people fall into the trap of believing their marriage will improve by just "trying harder" or by communicating their "needs" more effectively.

Celebration of Sex

The act of sex, an important portion of consummation, or yada, is sometimes called "making love" as if the physical action of our bodies can actually create or manufacture love. The better term is "expressing love," because love begins in our spirit, and is then manifested in our soul through intimate thoughts and feelings, and is then expressed with complete freedom through our bodies in the loving boundary of marriage.

Sex is a beautiful expression of love, and it was never meant to be shameful. By understanding the Father's heart and the beauty of His creation, the Jews are unashamed and celebrate the act of marriage during the wedding celebration. In Jewish tradition, the wedding celebration tarries several days and sometimes beyond a week. During the celebration, the bridal chamber is often connected to the venue of celebration. Typically, all that separates the newlyweds from their guests is a curtain. When the virgin couple consummates their marriage, there is usually blood on the bed sheet. The couple then throws the blood stained bed sheet (sign of the covenant) over the curtain and the crowd cheers and celebrates! Although this may be uncomfortable in our culture, sex in marriage is important and glorious and should be celebrated.

In our society and culture, sex outside of marriage is considered commonplace and normal. Even many Christians see premarital sex as "no big deal." However, it is not the way that we see it that is important, it is the way that He sees it. When a man "knows" a woman is goes much deeper than just a physical union, it is an actual consummation of two people. Remember, consummation means "yada."

The Father put loving boundaries around us so that we don't yada with the enemy. When we yada with a person that is not our spouse, we are open to the influence and the voice of the enemy. Not only have you "consumed" something against His instructions, but you have also opened yourself up to all the "stuff" that belongs to the sexual partner. Sexual intercourse is an act of covenant. Covenant means "All that I have is yours and all that you have mine" (1 Corinthians 6:15–17). You have not only slept with someone with whom you are not committed, submitted, and one-ified, but also have taken on all that they have. For too many, premarital sex is truly a vain attempt to "make love." They are desperate to feel affection, and they hope they can find it in giving themselves to another. They hope that they can ultimately feed their soul and spirit through their body, when it should be reverse. Premarital sex is a really big deal! It is always an act of desperation that leads to more desperation.

Conversely, sex within a marital relationship is meant to be extremely powerful and an act of deeper intimacy within consummation.

Sex in marriage should be viewed as the thermometer not the thermostat. We think that our marriage will become healthier if we just "turn up the heat" in the bedroom. However, your body doesn't feed your soul and spirit. It would be better to strengthen your spirit, which feeds your soul and your feelings. This will, in turn, I assure you, turn up the heat! Said in another way, if your sex life is cold, turn to your identity in Him and in your marriage as one flesh. Allow your spirit to speak to your soul about your spouse. When this happens, your mind, emotions, and feelings toward your spouse will come alive and so will your body!

Shame and Hiding

Shame is an ugly word. It is the first manifestation of sin and is responsible for the loss of the beautiful original culture. Not surprisingly, the roots of the word shame are thought to derive from an older word meaning "to cover." So, covering oneself, literally or figuratively, is a natural expression of shame. Shame is an emotion of reflected self-assessment. This reflected self-assessment always leaves you hiding and covered.

You see, nakedness is not a sin—it is part of the Father's culture, which He called "good." But, upon self-assessment, we feel shame, which results in a fallen perception of nakedness, and we create for ourselves coverings to hide ourselves from our spouses. Does that sound familiar? The events in the garden took place thousands of years ago, and yet nothing has changed.

On a side note, I feel shame is such an ugly word that the expression "shame on you" should be considered equal to "go to hell" or "damn you." It is one of the most sinister and devastating tools of the enemy. In my opinion, after my studies of Genesis and the heart of the Father, to say "shame on you" is the equivalent of a curse and should be removed from a Christian's vocabulary.

Shame does not respect time, person, or denomination. Shame attaches itself to the young and the old, the rich and the poor, the Christian and the heathen, the offender and the victim. The enemy doesn't really care; he just wants you in shame!

Intricate Coverings

If we are honest, we all have crafted quite intricate coverings. Many in the church today may even see shame as appropriate, honorable, and justified. For some, shame has become a familiar friend. There is such a sense of guilt and disqualification that living in hiding seems like the safest place in the world. Shame is also the byproduct of judgment and anger from others. Some even call it justice. This keeps people locked in shame.

We cover ourselves and hide to keep people from getting too close to us. When we examine all of the traditional problems in marriage—lack of communication, anger, criticism, moodiness, distraction, and abuse—we notice that they are all defense mechanisms designed to keep others away. Again, these aren't the problems; they are the symptoms. When someone raises their voice, becomes red in the face, and shakes their fist, it tends to back everyone down. When someone is moody or crabby, it doesn't exactly make you want to cuddle with them, and that's the whole point. Most everyone learns how to communicate by the age of three, so don't tell me couples don't know *how* to communicate with each other. Couples don't communicate with each other because they don't *want* to! They want to keep each other at a safe distance. They are uncomfortable with transparency, and the last thing they want to do is share their guarded, hidden, shameful hearts with each other.

Transparency is not something that comes easily for me, and generally speaking, it can be more difficult for men. I am not only a man, I am a private one, and I enjoy peace and quiet and tend to refuel in solitude. Remember the eight kids? Needless to say, quiet is not always easy to find. Despite this, the Holy Spirit compels me to be more open and transparent with my wife. I will confess I feel somewhat clumsy at times, but because it is His culture, and I have value for His heart and my wife's heart, I will continue this journey.

As long as you're covered, intimacy will be lost. As long as you're hiding, your marriage will be ineffective. So what do we do? Let's start by asking: What is the purpose of a covering? It is to keep you from seeing me. It keeps me from being transparent. It keeps you from seeing who I really am...and once again, it is an issue of identity.

Don't move past identity. Pursue your identity until you can look at yourself in the mirror and say without a shadow of doubt, "I am a loved son or daughter of the most high God!" This is where it has to begin. As long as you stay an orphan, and resist the Father's love, you will never be able to pursue true intimacy in your marriage. Once you see yourself as royalty and believe you are unconditionally loved, then, and only then, will you feel comfortable to come out of the shadows and truly be seen by your spouse.

The final critical step is to remove all of those coverings, overcome shame, and embrace intimacy!

We Can't Do It

If this is the ultimate goal, to remove the coverings, how do we do it? Shame put them there, how do we get rid of them? The answer is, *we can't!*

Remember, this has to be a job for our spirit. It has nothing to do with our bodies or physical clothing, or our simple willpower (soul). Shame can only be overcome through spiritual healing. Thus, it must be a work of the Holy Spirit. Only the Holy Spirit can bring true freedom. The opposite of shame is freedom. Freedom is a culture of the reflected Holy Spirit assessment that removes coverings and leaves you unashamed!

In John 16:7 Jesus says one of the most provocative things: "Nevertheless, I tell you the truth. It is to your advantage that I go away; for if I do not go away, the Helper will not come to you." Again, He is referring to the Holy Spirit, and if Jesus thinks that it's to our advantage that He goes away, the Holy Spirit must be pretty awesome! In fact, He really is, and the advantage is that, instead of God with us, we receive God in us. The Holy Spirit is so loving and gentle, and his sole purpose is to transform us into the image of Christ. If we will allow Him, He will do a masterful job at identifying, naming, and eliminating the shame in your life. The Holy Spirit has given us a gift, whereby if used, will result in unprecedented freedom. The name of that gift is repentance.

A Good Gift

I believe that repentance is completely misunderstood. We often think of it as a payment, an apology, or painful groveling. But rather, it is a gift through the Holy Spirit. Therefore, it is never a negative work. The Bible says that repentance is a good gift of God, not a good work we do for God (Acts 5:31, 11:18, 2 Timothy 2:25). Repentance is not a call to groveling or penance; rather, repentance is a call to intimacy.

True repentance is running to the Father instead of hiding from the Father. That is exactly what we need! This stems from the revelation that our loving Father is not ashamed of us, nor does He want us to be ashamed of us! Remember, shame is never a part of His plan. Shame is not the new order; it is the *out of order*!

Repentance means to change the way you think. I have had to repent to the Father because I "thought" I needed to hide from Him, and the coverings I put around my heart were to keep Him from seeing me. Becoming a son has allowed me to change the way I think about Him as the Father. Repentance has allowed me to remove the coverings of shame and enter His kingdom naked and free.

Similarly, repentance has allowed me to change the way I think about my spouse. I assumed my wife appreciated all my coverings. They were intricate and well designed. If I could conceal my shame and insecurities, then all she would have to see is the relatively decent exterior of who I am. What I discovered on this journey is that my wife is for me and not against me. She is my one flesh, not my enemy. I found out that my wife actually wants to see me naked! I will continue to allow the Holy Spirit to identify and remove the coverings that hinder me from the intimacy we both desire!

The culture of Eden has been restored through the blood of Jesus. So let's once again run into the loving arms of the Father; allow the Holy Spirit to transform your spirit. Run to Him with the spirit of repentance and allow the Holy Spirit to remove the coverings! It will be the greatest transformation and restoration of intimacy in your marriage.

Repentance and forgiveness require courage. I fully understand that there have been real mistakes, real hurt, real pain, real betrayal, real disappointment, real abuse, and real sorrow in marriages. To allow the Holy Spirit access to your heart, you will require real vulnerability. However, your marriage is worth it!

No matter what state your marriage is currently in, from solid to in shambles, your marriage is worth this greater pursuit of intimacy. The enemy has kept shame and coverings in your life long enough, but he is already defeated, and he will be defeated in every attempt to keep you in hiding.

So ask the Holy Spirit. It can really be that simple. The Holy Spirit isn't fragile. In fact, he's all-powerful and certainly isn't afraid of the tactics of the devil. However, he does offer us free will. He will never force himself on you. This will have to be your choice; you just have to want it.

Ask the Holy Spirit to show you where you have created coverings in your marriage. Ask Him to replace the lies you have believed with the truth. Then, joyfully pursue repentance and ask the Holy Spirit to remove the coverings and restore the culture of marriage that is naked and unashamed.

Get Naked

This is my last simple, yet profound, truth: everything gets better in marriage the more naked you get! This is the only way to truly know each other, the way the Father intended.

What was lost has been restored! The ultimate pursuit for every marriage should be to restore the original culture of marriage. The original culture of marriage is "And they were both naked, the man and his wife, and were not ashamed." Remember, when we are unashamed, we can be naked, and when we are naked, we can be intimate! Coverings hinder intimacy and are created by shame.

Are you having problems feeling unified with your spouse? Do you never feel like you're on the same page? Then get naked!

Do you feel like your spouse has more fun with other people than with you? Do you wish you did more things together? I'm sure it would help if you were more naked!

Do you feel like you're always arguing? Do you feel like you're always criticizing or nagging? I have a solution for you—get naked!

I can even promise you this, your sex life will improve the more naked you get!

The more naked you are, the more oneness and intimacy you will feel. The more naked your spouse becomes, the more greatness and destiny you will see in them. Isn't that what we want in our marriages? Shame and coverings kill intimacy. Conversely, being naked and unashamed is exactly the culture the Father had in mind for every marriage! This is the consummation. This is a husband and wife being restored to the culture of Eden. This is the ultimate!

Conclusion

"Get Back" (to Where You Once Belonged)
The Beatles, 1969

We probably shouldn't be surprised that our loving Father created the world with the culture of heaven in mind. This is His culture, and His fingerprints are imprinted on all of creation. However, we may be surprised to learn that marriage is actually a crowning jewel of this demonstration. He sent His Son, Jesus, to the earth to save us, to offer us the right to once again become His children and to be joined to Him as his bride. Incredibly, He also wants us to be commissioned, operate in submission, become one with Him, and become deeply intimate with the bridegroom, the lover of our soul. This is *the ultimate* relationship we can truly ever experience!

Furthermore, our loving Father creates an earthly relationship that directly reflects His heavenly heart. He joins husbands and wives together to reflect the culture of heaven here on earth. So, when we pursue the fullness of a culture that He creates for us, what He calls "good," we too can experience the *ultimate* marriage.

As stated in the introduction, this book was never intended to be a "to-do list," with the goal of having you just try harder, with your own strength and soul, to fix or improve your marriage. I hope by now you have come to terms with the fact that you cannot fix your marriage. Only the Holy Spirit can. Hopefully, this book has given you targets in your marriage that you can bring before the Holy Spirit and allow Him to do the work.

This book takes you through the depths of intimacy that are, in a sense, chronological, or better stated, it gives you some starting points on your journey to the ultimate depth of intimacy where you and your spouse will be naked and unashamed. However, this book is not intended to be a rigid step-by-step checklist that ultimately gets you to your destination. The Holy Spirit is often not linear or predictable in the path or process that he will take in your marriage. But I am confident the Holy Spirit will always take you to a greater place of healing and intimacy, and the end goal will always be the Father's original heart!

With that being said, the first step always needs to be identity. We have to know who we are and whose we are. We have to get to the point where we can look at ourselves in the mirror and confidently say, "I am a loved son or daughter of the most high God." If we try to fix or advance our marriages as an orphan, disappointment will ensue. However long it takes, no matter your age, or however long you have been married, start with identity. This has been the single most important transformation in our marriage and family, and it will be for you, too. You may need to find those around you to pray for you and to hold you accountable in your identity. You can only afford to think about yourself the way the Father thinks about you.

This process will be so transformational as you begin to solidify your worth, value, and identity as a son or daughter, which in turn, will end the vicious cycle of having to look to others, including your spouse, to meet your needs. I can testify that this will bring such peace and alignment to your marriage.

I highly recommend, when the time is right, that you look your spouse in the eye and say, "I'm sorry for asking you to carry something that was never yours to carry. I release you from the burden to meet my needs and form my identity."

Next, it is time to rekindle your commissioning. Most of us, if we are honest, probably married as orphans. We didn't pay a lot of attention to *why* we were getting married. It is clear that the Father's original culture for marriage is infused with purpose and destiny. We, as married couples, have a mission. There are things that can only be done together, and that is why He created *them*.

It may be helpful to spend time with your spouse and take a "walk through memory lane." Remember back to when you first met. Recall the feelings, hopes, dreams, and passion that you had for each other. Also, ask the Holy Spirit to restore the purpose and plan for your marriage. Ask him to restore clarity of vision, without the obscuring lens of the orphan spirit. Ask the Father why He brought you together in the first place. It is never too late! He is a God of restoration. Your time together is too valuable to live with the regret of time lost. Rather, pursue the Father's heart for your marriage and for each other, and watch your unity of purpose ignite!

Once He has reignited your mission, it will be critical that you, together, become subject to the mission. Your marriage needs to be the proper demonstration of the Biblical mandate to be submissive to one another. It is from this spirit that husbands and wives can operate in honor of each other, and give each other authority to speak into their lives. There will be incredible breakthroughs and power demonstrated in your relationship, when you operate in equal and comparable strength as husband and wife. True submission means that you are "all in."

I recommend, when the time is right, that you look your spouse in the eye, and say, "I am subject to our mission and to the mission of our family. I give you authority to speak into my life. When it comes to our marriage and family, I am all in."

When the spirit of commission and submission is restored to your marriage, you'll have a platform to dive even deeper into intimacy. The two people that existed prior to your wedding no longer exist. You are transformed into someone who is completely unique. The only demonstration on earth of this process of one-ification is marriage. Your spouse does not complete you; your spouse is you! You are one flesh; the Bible cannot be clearer.

When we embrace our oneness, then and only then, we will see our spouse not as a threat or competition but as our double portion. The culture of our marriage will shift when we stop ruling over each other and start being one.

I recommend, when the time is right, that you look your spouse in the eye and say, "You and I are one. You are not my competition, not a threat, not my enemy; you are for me, not against me. You are me! I receive you as a double portion, all that I have in addition to all that you have."

Finally, we can pursue the ultimate, the deepest place of intimacy, created by our loving Father from the beginning of time. This is the place of consummation where we not only enjoy physical intimacy in marriage, or the feelings, and emotions for each other in our souls but also pursue the greatest experiences found in our spirit when we truly *know* each other! The greatest depth of intimacy is only found when the culture of Eden, where they were naked and unashamed, is restored. This culture goes way beyond their bodies or souls; it is a spiritual cultural reality intended for every marriage.

This will require vulnerability, not only with each other but also with the Holy Spirit. It will only be the Holy Spirit that lovingly exposes the coverings of shame and gently removes them. We need to be baptized in the Father's love, so whenever we feel shame, we will run *to* Him, not hide *from* Him! When we joyfully pursue this true repentance, the culture of our marriages will be restored.

I recommend, when the time is right, that you look your spouse in the eye and say, "I commit to nakedness. I will regularly ask the Holy Spirit if I have any coverings of shame that keep me hiding from you or from Him. I will ask the Holy Spirit to remove those coverings so that you can truly *know* me. I am no longer satisfied with a marriage that the world calls 'good.' I am pursuing *the ultimate*, a marriage culture that *He* created and *He* calls good!"

Do you desire to learn more about family?
Check out Jonathan's book
Restoring the Power of Family
at
www.familyrestorationproject.com
or
Contact Jonathan at
claussen@familyrestorationproject.com

Made in the USA
Lexington, KY
03 July 2018